THE COLLEGE STRESS TEST

The College Stress Test

Tracking Institutional Futures across a Crowded Market

ROBERT ZEMSKY

SUSAN SHAMAN

SUSAN CAMPBELL BALDRIDGE

JOHNS HOPKINS UNIVERSITY PRESS
Baltimore

© 2020 Johns Hopkins University Press
All rights reserved. Published 2020
Printed in the United States of America on acid-free paper
9 8 7 6 5 4 3 2 1

Johns Hopkins University Press
2715 North Charles Street
Baltimore, Maryland 21218-4363
www.press.jhu.edu

Library of Congress Cataloging-in-Publication Data

Names: Zemsky, Robert, 1940– author. | Shaman, Susan, author. | Baldridge,
    Susan Campbell, 1964– author.
Title: The college stress test : tracking institutional futures across a crowded market /
    Robert Zemsky, Susan Shaman, Susan Campbell Baldridge.
Description: Baltimore : Johns Hopkins University Press, 2020. |
    Includes bibliographical references and index.
Identifiers: LCCN 2019025619 | ISBN 9781421437033 (hardcover) |
    ISBN 9781421437040 (ebook)
Subjects: LCSH: Universities and colleges—United States—Business management. |
    Universities and colleges—United States—Evaluation. | College choice—Economic
    aspects—United States.
Classification: LCC LB2341.93.U6 Z46 2020 | DDC 378.1/06—dc23
LC record available at https://lccn.loc.gov/2019025619

A catalog record for this book is available from the British Library.

*Special discounts are available for bulk purchases of this book. For more information,
please contact Special Sales at specialsales@press.jhu.edu.*

Johns Hopkins University Press uses environmentally friendly book materials,
including recycled text paper that is composed of at least 30 percent post-consumer
waste, whenever possible.

CONTENTS

This volume would not have been possible without Rick Morgan. He built our database from carefully documented IPEDS (Integrated Postsecondary Education Data System) extractions. He edited all of our drafts. And most important, he kept checking our work for consistency and accuracy. He has all of our thanks.

We benefited as well by the access four presidents granted to their institutions: Laura Casamento of Utica College, Teresa Dreyfuss of Rio Hondo Community College, Mark Putnam of Central College, and Marcia Welsh of Eastern Stroudsburg University. It was their and their staff's willingness to try out the metrics we were developing that gave us confidence that we were on the right track. Presidents Putnam and Casamento also read portions of our draft and contributed writings of their own that buttressed our conclusions.

In the prologue we tell the story of how Greg Britton of Johns Hopkins University Press gave us the idea for this volume. His colleague Catherine Goldstead shepherded the manuscript (made unforgivingly complex by the inclusion of more than 70 figures and tables) through the Press's processes and procedures. Our final text was copyedited by Andre Barnett, who almost always allowed us to leave our idiosyncrasies embedded in the text.

Finally, we drew on the work of a coterie of gifted graduate students from University of Pennsylvania's Executive Doctorate in Higher Education Management Program. We benefited even more directly from the dissertations of three of these students: Andrew Armitage of the University of the Sciences, Laura Casamento of Utica College, and Peggy McCready of Northwestern University. Kimberly Sluis of North Central College provided a critically important read of the near final manuscript. Karen Vahey of the New York Institute of Technology added an important interview.

All of these friends, students, and colleagues were more than generous; the errors in this volume, however, are ours alone.

THE COLLEGE STRESS TEST

Is It Closing Time?

S HE WAS BOTH A SENIOR administrator and an advanced graduate
student in the University of Pennsylvania's Executive Doctorate in
Higher Education Program. And she had had enough. Another four-
hour graduate class focusing on market mechanics was more than a
bridge too far. "Why," she sputtered, "are we always talking about the
market? Why not talk about ideals and values, about aspirations and
expectations, about the societal barriers that deny so many a higher
education that is worth something?" She wasn't alone. Hers were frus-
trations shared by many. Given their druthers, those most responsible
for the fate of the nation's colleges and universities would rather talk
about almost anything else, having concluded that talking about the
market only diminishes the enterprise.

Still, as both teaching faculty and seasoned administrators, we have
persisted, convinced that understanding the market holds the key to
gauging what the future holds for American higher education. We
understand that focusing on how that market functions puts us in the
same company with those who would forecast a dismal future for the
industry. Theirs is the sense that the enterprise is already in decline.
What lies ahead, these modern-day Cassandras gladly proclaim, is
an era of disruptive change yielding a future that is both wasteful and
chaotic. It will be a future of shuttered institutions, of colleges and

universities that, having lost their competitive edge, have no choice but to close. While the wealthiest schools, with their endowments and oversubscribed applicant pools, should feel safe enough, their claim is that nearly every other institution needs to be concerned about its long-term viability.

Taking these concerns seriously leads to an interesting question: Might it be possible to know now which institutions are most at risk of failing in the future—either closing outright or being absorbed by another, more successful provider? The answer, we decided, was yes, provided there was at hand a means for calibrating the market stresses each institution is likely to face.

We hope that the book you have before you does exactly that. Our interest in understanding how and when institutions are likely to close began with an earlier exploration of the market for a legal education in the United States. We had been invited by the AccessLex Institute to explore how a 20 percent contraction in the market for a law degree was likely to change American legal education, given a mounting surplus of unfilled places in the entering classes at the nation's law schools. We started with a pair of labels borrowed from meteorologists; the possibility of an approaching storm is identified as a storm "watch" (or alert), and then, as it becomes apparent that dangerously bad weather is imminent, a watch becomes a storm "warning." We recast these terms to signal an impending law school admissions market *alert* and subsequently an admissions market *warning*. The highly structured market for legal education in the United States made it possible to construct a model that used changes over time in just five variables—(1) an institution's market price, (2) first-year attrition, (3) mean LSAT score, (4) bar passage rate, and (5) employment in a JD-required position after graduation—to predict whether a given law school was likely to encounter serious market stress. What proved important was not the actual percentage of students who dropped out in their first year of law school but, rather, the slope of the line describing changes in that metric over time. That is, the rate of change in first-year law student attrition for a given school could serve as one of the handful of indicators that predicted worse outcomes, not the actual amount of attrition.

This analysis drew the attention of Greg Britton of Johns Hopkins University Press, who asked whether we had considered developing a similar market stress test to project the futures of *undergraduate* institutions across the United States. Upon reviewing the available data, what we came to understand was that the methodology we had developed to make sense of the contracting market for a legal education in the United States did have, as Britton had surmised, general applicability to other education markets.

We started with the market structure presented in *The Market Imperative* (Zemsky and Shaman 2017) and, as in that volume, used the institutional data available from IPEDS (Integrated Postsecondary Education Data System) to cast a set of metrics for estimating the market viability of more than 2,800 undergraduate institutions. We first mapped the contour-changing shifts that facilitate rich institutions getting richer, while institutions at the bottom are being hollowed out. When they have nothing left to hold on to, they think about closing.

We focused next on predicting the distribution of undergraduate enrollments, both for four- and two-year institutions. For this analysis, we used a different set of variables than we had used in our law school study but retained our insight that we could best describe an institution's market future in terms of the degree to which those metrics changed over time for each institution.

The final stage of our analysis yielded two summary mappings of institutional stress test scores. The first identified the characteristics of the institutions facing the greatest stress based on a listing of the institutions with the highest Market Stress Test Scores. The second summary mapping focused on the demographic (ethnicity, gender, age, economic status) characteristics of the students served in each of the market's sectors and segments. This mapping yielded a listing of the categories of students most often served by institutions experiencing moderate to severe market stress, which, in turn, yielded a more precise estimate of the students who are most commonly served by institutions experiencing the greatest market stress.

A traditional statistical analysis of a phenomenon such as institutional closings might have employed a logistic regression or similar model to estimate the probability of closing using data from institutions that have closed and those that remain active. The model's parameter estimates would have been applied to currently active institutions to predict the probability of their closing. That, however, was not a strategy we could use. There simply were not enough closed institutions, and those few that have closed were almost exclusively from the bottom of the market.

At its core, this effort to identify institutions at greatest risk due to shifting student markets is a quantitative one. We wanted to know which institutions were most at risk of closing and why. But we believe it is also important to understand the emotions that inevitably swirl around questions of institutional viability. So, we start this volume with the language of closing itself—the words and concepts being used to describe potentially gloomy futures. Much of that language is frankly funereal, as in *The Atlantic* piece headlined, "Here's How Higher Education Dies" (Harris 2018). Nothing noble or particularly enriching in that phrase, but in ways that surprised us, it set the tone for understanding what we are really about. In the pages that follow, we begin with an initial chapter exploring the language of institutional viability, risk, and failure and then describe how the market has already shifted, before presenting the results of our market stress test analysis. We conclude with our own sense of how the future is likely to play out and how an individual institution might assess and reconsider its future.

ONE

Threat, Reassurance, and Grief

Estimating the number of colleges or universities about to close has become something of a national parlor game. The guesses need to be well argued as well as scary, and the headlines that accompany their public release are expected to stress the latter more than the former. An early entrant was Tom Frey, blogger, featured speaker, and self-described futurist. "We are trusting colleges to instill valuable knowledge in our students, and in doing so, create a more valuable workforce and society," Frey noted in a 2013 blog post. "But when those who find no tangible value begin to openly proclaim, 'the emperor has no clothes!' colleges will find themselves in a hard-to-defend downward spiral." By his reckoning, what higher education had to look forward to was an era marked by a "mass failure of traditional colleges." How many would actually close? Frey's headline had the answer: "By 2030 over 50% of Colleges Will Collapse" (Frey 2013).

Frey's prediction was just one. Other commentators, including Clayton Christensen, Harvard Business School professor, predicted the same outcome but far sooner. From the financial corner, Moody's Investors Service predicted that the rate of college closings and forced mergers would more than triple by 2017. When that date came and went without the prophecy being realized, Moody's, like the end-of-the-world predictors of the nineteenth century, reanalyzed and predicted that the college closing rate would still triple but in the near future rather than in the immediate present (Seltzer 2018a). And while others were less specific about numbers and dates, the crystal ball seemed to show a dismal future indeed.

What we know now is that these predictions weren't entirely off the mark; there will be institutions that close or are forced into mergers because they have run out of money. The rate of closings has already increased but only slightly. Although mass closings are not imminent, new notices of colleges in distress are appearing with alarming frequency, and conversations about the risks that underenrolled and underfunded institutions now face are changing the higher education narrative. For those not currently in dire circumstances, what is emerging is the need for an uncomfortable but nonetheless necessary conversation about market risks and the possibility of institution failures.

The task we have set for ourselves, then, is providing a metric for estimating those risks. We have developed a methodology for evaluating the highest risk sectors within higher education and for estimating risk for individual institutions. But we understand that numbers, in and of themselves, may persuade almost no one who doesn't already believe that the sky is falling. To understand and then to make use of the numbers require a better understanding of the context in which those numbers will be viewed—by the policy wonks who influence federal and state policies and budgets; by those in the press whose writings often shape the narrative; and, most particularly, by those with institutional responsibilities who know they must now navigate a changed landscape.

Thus, we begin with a consideration of three different, and largely disconnected, conversations taking place about higher education and its future. The first conversation, led by pundits, journalists, and cultural commentators, is occurring in the media and is a story that focuses on the looming threat to higher education. The arguments hinge on changing demographics, institutional cultures resistant to change, and failures of leadership. The predictions are often dire, pointing to mass closures and mergers and to looming risk that calls for a reconsideration of the very enterprise itself. A second set of conversations are taking place on college and university campuses and in the offices of presidents and provosts trying to determine where their own institutions stand in this landscape of risk. The campus conversations focus on a particular school's history, traditions, opportunities, and challenges and are calibrated to reassure faculty, staff, students, alumni, and parents that College X is well poised to respond to the needs of today's and tomorrow's students. In private, presidents and other institutional leaders are trying to determine what the real risk is—not for the industry as a whole but for their particular institutions—and how to respond to it without eliciting active resistance among their constituents or scaring away next year's much-needed applicants. The third set of conversations largely involve the campus communities of institutions that have closed. They are conversations of grief and remorse, as well as puzzlement as to "why us?"

In the balance of this chapter, we describe these often distinct conversations, trying to reconcile them with one another as a prelude to our analyses of the distribution of measurable risk and probability of actual closing.

The Language of Industry-Wide Threat: The Sky Is Falling

For about a decade, likely precipitated by the financial earthquake that rocked most colleges and universities during the Great Recession, the conversation about the dismal fate of higher education has been gaining steam. Probably the best-known prognosticator is Clayton Christensen, the Harvard Business School professor who had previously argued that a decade or more of disruptive innovation in manufacturing had already upended the established order of that economic sector. Turning his attention to the world of higher education, he argued that new online education innovations and career-focused credential programs were disrupting the industry, responding to current market needs and opportunities in a way that legacy schools were not. Higher education was, he argued, "on the edge of the crevasse" (Howe 2013).

Those schools that failed to innovate in response to changing market demands were going to be left behind, mastodons braying in the tar pit. As a result, he said, traditional colleges and universities that failed to innovate would not survive, and as many as half of all colleges and universities would be bankrupt or closed within a decade. Not surprisingly, it was a prediction that garnered a lot of attention. Asked recently whether he stood by this estimate he replied, "If you're asking whether the providers get disrupted within a decade—I might bet it takes nine years rather than 10" (Lederman 2017).

Christensen's is a prediction based in theory—his own disruptive innovation theory. Other commentators have made similar predictions about the changing higher education landscape, based instead on demographic data about the college-going population. Author and journalist Jeff Selingo, for example, has described changing demographics in the United States that have the potential to create "a supply and demand crisis." He points to anticipated declines in the number of high school graduates, including particular decreases in the number of college-bound students in New England and the Midwest, and a more racially and ethnically diverse college applicant pool nationwide. Add to this the challenge for most students and their families of paying for a college education, even with some amount of aid. "That means colleges won't have much of an ability to raise prices in the future," he says, "putting more pressure on them to cut costs, develop different pricing models or build entirely new models for the traditional four-year residential college" (Selingo 2018). Nathan Grawe, an economist at Carleton College in Minnesota, has similarly analyzed these demographic shifts, using the data to highlight the need for future innovations that speak to the needs of the market. Although he predicts that elite colleges like his own will fare reasonably well, he nonetheless uses fairly dramatic imagery about the coming future for most of higher ed, especially "the end of the 2020s when enrollments are in free fall" (Jaschik 2018).

Other forecasters of the coming storm have simply been observing trends in higher education over the past decade, noting shifts in a number of domains that portend a challenging future for many colleges.

Bryan Alexander, author and futurist, described the state of the industry in 2013 as "peak higher ed." Akin to "peak car" and "peak oil," Alexander claimed that "peak higher ed means we've reached the maximum size that colleges and universities can support. What we see now . . . is as big as it gets. After two generations of growth, American higher education has reached its upper bound." The consequence is an industry that will have to rightsize, meaning the elimination of the most vulnerable schools. In an *Atlantic* interview, Alexander says, "The business model for a lot of colleges is dependent on enrollment. If enrollments decline [. . .], that creates a sort of death spiral in which colleges are getting rid of programs, which in turn makes it harder to attract students, and so on" (Harris 2018). The death spiral imagery is dramatic but captures the tone of many of these prophecies.

Another contribution to the public conversation about the fate of higher education comes in the form of reporting on specific schools that have announced that they are closing or seeking a merger partner. These accounts are often largely focused on explaining the college's fate through an examination of its particulars. When Mount Ida, a small college in Massachusetts, announced that it was closing, the focus was on the process by which the decision was made and whether its financial status should have been disclosed sooner by its president (Carapezza 2018). When the newly appointed president of financially challenged Earlham College announced he was stepping down, journalists raised questions about the circumstances surrounding that decision: What was the board's involvement, and were governance processes followed? (Mangan 2018). Another investigative piece examining documents related to the accreditation status of Saint Augustine's University challenged the claims of the school's leaders that financial conditions were improving (Seltzer 2018b). Then there is the detailed account of the almost closure and then rescue of Sweet Briar College, brought back from the brink by deeply committed alumni and donors (although, even in this case, the writer notes that "survival is still no sure thing"; Lindsay 2018). These post hoc and posthumous microanalyses seem to foreshadow the predicted demise of the industry.

And whatever the particulars surrounding a school in trouble, journalists indeed portray these cases as a window onto the future for other schools. The headline on one near-bankrupt college's announcement of likely closure read "Iowa Wesleyan's Fate Underscores Woes Facing Others" (Miller 2018). Another article summarizing several small college closures described these as "days of reckoning" (Seltzer 2017). Another account notes the "uptick in college closures" under the headline "The College Bubble Begins to Deflate" (Leef 2018). Increasingly, the views expressed in these pieces are beginning to align with the predictions of the prognosticators: these particular cases are seen as harbingers of hardship for the industry more generally.

Thus, the public conversation suggests a gloomy future for colleges and universities. The story these journalists and prognosticators tell varies in its origins and underpinnings—whether it emerges from theory, demographic data, an analysis of broader education trends, or accounts of the particular schools whose fate has already been sealed. But the message is the same in all cases: higher education is on the brink of crisis, and schools need to sit up and take notice.

The Language of Institutional Reassurance: "Everything's Gonna Be Alright"

While journalists are devoting increasing column inches to their gloomy forecasts, the conversation taking place on most college and university campuses is noticeably different. In fact, if you diagnosed the well-being of higher education based on the public comments and missives of presidents around the country, you would conclude that the patient is largely in good health. Most such accounts have a fairly positive outlook to offer: College X is thriving. University Y is optimistic about the future. School Z is redirecting efforts with a bold new strategy. These messages intentionally link the school's distinctive history and mission with a promise of exciting opportunities and long-term vibrancy.

For example, one college unveiling its strategic plan announced: "The plan reaffirms [our] distinctive strengths, identifies opportunities to advance our mission, and provides the framework to support our aspiration to be a national model for liberal arts education" (Dudley 2018). Similarly, one university provost launched a strategic plan proclaiming that "our goal [is] to be nothing less than *the* great research university of the 21st century. I hope you'll see it as I do: A vision for this university in which we are encouraged and supported to work, teach, and study to the very best of our ability" (Quick 2018). This kind of language is entirely reasonable, given the largely internal audience at which it is directed. It is the job of presidents and provosts to create enthusiasm and buy-in for whatever strategic change is being sought. But in contrast to the broader conversation about risk and threats to the industry, note that the language is unfailingly positive and that the message begins with the prospect of a bright institutional future.

Does this mean that those who are responsible for leading our colleges and universities are so many Pollyannas, unaware of the larger conversation about the future of higher education? Unlikely. Most higher ed leaders, at least privately, acknowledge the critics and the dire predictions, but their response is often that those in higher ed simply need to make a better case for the value of the enterprise. Survey after survey of education leaders points to a strongly held belief that the public does not understand the purpose of what colleges and universities do. When asked about higher education's future, Harvard President Larry Bacow recently said, "People are questioning the value of a diploma. They are questioning the value of these institutions to society. They are questioning whether or not colleges and universities actually contribute to the American dream. That's scary. We need to change that conversation" (Walsh 2018). Thus, a common response to predictions of a dire future is to suggest that today's challenges emerge largely from problems of public perception. The prescription seems to be to try to create an alternate narrative—one that reminds people of the intellectual rewards and long-term financial value that results from higher education, especially liberal education.

Not all responses to doubts about the industry focus broadly on the value of higher education, however. A common focus of campus messaging is on the particular data points that suggest that, whatever risks may be facing other schools, the future for *my* college is bright. The point would seem to be to reassure constituents that, in the landscape of higher education, one's own school is well positioned to withstand today's threats. Thus, presidents' communications are far more likely to share the good news that applications are up this fall or to highlight the positive publicity received by a recent graduate, than they are to speak to potential threats to long-term viability.

This language of optimism and reassurance is understandable. Addressing threats to the sustainability of an institution requires persistent hard work by many, and a panicked community isn't likely to be able to respond effectively. What's more, if there is anxiety within the leadership ranks, it would not benefit anyone to acknowledge it. Much of the work of recruiting, enrolling, and retaining students—to say nothing of fund-raising—is about building reputations and managing the public's perception of an institution's desirability, prestige, and credibility. Potential students and donors are not likely to open their checkbooks to an institution whose future appears shaky. So, a struggling institution's leaders may wait to publicly acknowledge that reality until the very last hope for recovery has faded.

Whatever the pressures on leaders to publicly spread their school's good news, what do we know about what they are thinking privately and discussing with colleagues behind closed doors? As one indication, let's look at the findings of *Inside Higher Ed*'s annual anonymous survey of college and university presidents in 2019. The results suggest that many presidents are generally aware of the risks to the industry at large, and some—"nearly one in seven"—are worried that their own school may be at risk for closing or merging in the next five years. Nonetheless, the trend in these perceptions over time is increasingly positive. "Presidents express[ed] more confidence in the 10-year financial stability of their campuses than they have at any point in the last six years." They go on to report that "fifty-seven percent of presidents are confident in their institution's financial sustainability over a decade, up from 53 percent last year. Leaders of private four-year colleges are most confident (64 percent), public master's and baccalaureate college presidents the least (49 percent)." While these results acknowledge some level of worry among institutional leaders, the trends suggest that, in contrast to the pundits, most are coming to imagine a rosier future, rather than a darker one (Lederman 2019).

Inside Higher Ed's annual surveys of college and university chief business officers and admissions officers in 2018 also showed awareness and anxiety about the sustainability of some institutions, especially when it comes to meeting enrollment targets. "Just 44 percent of chief financial officers at four-year baccalaureate colleges say they are confident their college will be financially stable over the next 10 years, down from 52 percent a year ago and 54 percent in 2016." But while there are signs of growing concern over recent years, *Inside Higher Ed* notes that the shift "should not be overstated. For every answer that suggests that chief business officers recognize major problems, you can find another that shouts, 'No worries, we're good.' Contradictions abound" (Lederman 2018).

How to make sense of these contradictions? These survey results suggest that, at least on an intellectual level, many of these leaders are aware of the broader industry-wide concerns. Nonetheless, only a few are openly connecting the public conversation with their on-campus discussions. Some leaders *are* trying to communicate in a way that simultaneously acknowledges industry realities and expresses institutional optimism. A dean at one university wrote to her campus that "these are challenging times for the higher education community. . . . Declining or stagnant state support, increasing costs of attendance, shifting demographics and the perceived value of a 'liberal education' all have a major impact on our community. I have tremendous confidence that we have the commitment and talent to overcome all of these challenges and achieve our vision" (Koretsky 2017). But this is a fine rhetorical line to walk—balancing both risk and opportunity as the context for necessary change—and an educational community committed to their particular institution may not be receptive to this kind of nuance.

Perhaps no one should be surprised by the disconnect, then, between newspaper headlines and presidential rhetoric. Those whose careers and identities are tied up in leading an institution to thrive will naturally find it difficult to accept and acknowledge that the risk is real for their school. What's more, a closing has implications for a broad community of constituents, none of whom is likely to take such news lightly. After all, students and alumni are encouraged to develop an almost romantic affection for their alma maters. It can be very difficult to reconcile this kind of deeply rooted attachment for an institution with objective threats to that institution's survival. The challenge in reconciling these two narratives is thus explained by the very real emotions that connect the people in an educational community to their colleges and universities. Nowhere are those emotions more evident than in the narratives surrounding those colleges or universities that have already closed.

The Language of Elegiac Grief: "It Is with a Heavy Heart . . ."

An analysis of language used to describe institutional closures resembles the language of grief on learning of a loved one's sudden and unexpected passing. When the news spread in 2015 that Sweet Briar College would be closing (a decision that was ultimately reversed), the *Washington Post* described the response among one alumna's family: "It was like we were mourning a family member" (Svrluga 2016). About another college closure, *Inside Higher Ed* noted that "on social media, Green Mountain alumni mourned the college, noting qualities about it they loved" (Jaschik 2019). A student at Bennett College, on hearing the announcement that her school's accreditation was being rescinded: "It was a heavy feeling when we heard the news. This is a beloved institution, and nobody wants to think about it not being open" (Osei 2019). And when Dowling College abruptly announced it was shutting its doors, one alumna reminisced online as if a speaker at a memorial service: "Very sad to see an institution that was a big part of my life for four years close its doors. Still remember my first day as a freshman, walking past the well, and my last day, graduating on the lawn by the river. . . . And all the memories, and great friends that made my Dowling experience special" (Booth and

Bolger 2016). When emotional connections are this deep and strongly felt, the pressure to maintain the belief in an institution's good health and prosperity is significant.

If the metaphor of grief applies, then one can also listen for instances of the well-known stages of a mourning process. One hears something akin to denial in the tortuous language that leaders of threatened institutions feel compelled to employ when delivering genuinely bad news. In the following 2019 excerpt from a letter to the Hampshire College community from its president—who has since resigned, along with her board chair—it is unclear whether this is an announcement of possible closure or the kickoff to an exciting capital campaign:

> I'm announcing today our intent to find a long-term partner that can help us achieve a thriving and sustainable future for Hampshire. With the guidance and passion of Hampshire's trustees we've begun a process to seek a strategic partnership to address the challenges we've faced as an under-endowed institution, really from our very first days. . . . In November, we announced our plans to envision Hampshire's next half-century as we approach our 50th anniversary in 2020. *What will Hampshire's future look like?* is how we've framed the initiative, keeping top of mind that we would define what we treasure most about this special college—our mission, values, character—and leapfrog into the future. (Nelson 2019)

After denial, come anger and bargaining, both of which can be heard in the public outcry following the announcement of an impending shutdown. The most public and dramatic example is found in the case of Sweet Briar College, whose 2015 leadership announced that the college was to close in the face of dropping enrollments and meager donations. "Anger fueled fund raising and the legal campaign, which both took formal shape in Saving Sweet Briar, a group that joined a legal effort to block the closure. Alumnae, who had been on rocky terms with administrators in recent years, felt betrayed." The language of the legal proceedings continued the metaphor of grief and bargaining: "This college does not need to die," one of the group's lawyers argued. "This college does not need to commit suicide. This college only needs to do what a well-run college does" (Lindsay 2018). That group ultimately succeeded in court and, along with new college leadership, raised the funds needed to keep their alma mater alive. Other closures have provoked equally negative reactions. The *Boston Globe* reported that "students and parents voiced deep anger and a sense of betrayal toward Mount Ida College on Tuesday at the first public meeting held since the school abruptly announced its closure 2½ weeks ago." One mother in a public hearing asked, "Why are you preying on our children, luring them to come to Mount Ida with non-existent money?" (Krantz 2018b). Elsewhere, "former Heald College students struck back against the school they believe betrayed them, plastering the outside with angry posters, with messages such as 'U Failed Us!'" (Jacobs 2015). Granted, some of this anger is the result of very real concerns, both pragmatic and financial. Students may be wondering, "Will I be able to transfer my credits elsewhere and graduate on time?" and alumni may be concerned about the value of their degree from a soon-to-be defunct school in the professional marketplace. Nonetheless, such deep feelings of anger and betrayal suggest that, for many, college attendance is much more than a merely transactional exchange of money for credits.

Even postmortem analyses of schools that have ceased operations use the language of grief. One headline noted that "Former Mount Ida College Students and Staff Are Trying to Move Forward" (Krantz 2018a). In fact, if the death of a college or university ideally results in some form of acceptance, it would seem to be achieved through the belief that the ill-fated institution's example and mission will be remembered and carried on by others. The president of Green Mountain College concluded the college's obituary letter thusly: "We know that the spirit and mission of Green Mountain College will continue to live on in the lives of our graduates and broader community" (Allen 2019).

The fact that the language of institutional closure so closely parallels the well-understood stages of grief is all the evidence we need of people's affection for and connection to their particular college or university and of their belief in the exceptional nature of these institutions. In the character of this grief, then, we see the explanation for the disconnect between public conjectures about the dismal future of higher education and the more localized optimism about a particular school's immunity to the general malaise. It is precisely because each school matters so much to its people that conversations about risk are so hard to have. What is needed is a reconciliation between these two discourses, one that precedes the need for elegies and obituaries and, instead, points to the strategies for accurately diagnosing and acknowledging an institution's actual condition.

Until now, there have been few precise tools for identifying the schools most at risk. Indeed, from the vantage point of the president's office on any given campus, the general projection that half of all schools will be gone in a decade is not helpful for understanding one's own particular level of institutional risk, to say nothing of what to do about it. Likewise, journalistic postmortems that dwell on the specifics of another school's demise aren't likely to find broader traction, so accustomed are educational leaders to focusing on distinctive strengths and institutional uniqueness. (Indeed, schadenfreude is perhaps a more likely reaction.) To connect the public conversation—a general discussion of higher education as an industry at great risk—with the more localized efforts of leaders to highlight the opportunities ahead on their own campuses, those leaders need to understand where their institution resides in the landscape of risk. How real is the threat for their *particular* school? What are the objective indicators that would allow them to know whether their risk is minimal or substantial? Answering these questions is the purpose of this book.

TWO

A Winner's Market

I T's A FAIR QUESTION. Put most simply: Is American higher education now on the verge of a major contraction? That more people are
asking whether a college education is still worth the cost has rein-
forced the notion that the enterprise is now ripe for disruptive change.
The irony is that the numbers reflecting actual student enrollments suggest a different, less chaotic, but nonetheless tough, future for American
higher education. That understanding starts with recognizing that higher
education's most traditional market, which serves traditional-aged students pursuing a four-year baccalaureate degree, has been expanding at
roughly 1.1 percent per year, or by nearly 9 percent over the past eight
years. Even the market for a two-year degree was not much smaller in
2016 than it was in 2008, having returned to its prior levels following
an expansion during the 2007–2008 recession. The only sector of the
market that fits Clayton Christensen's prediction was served by for-
profit providers, a group of institutions in near free fall as the federal
government sought to rein in what had been a boom market financed
by Washington, DC's own largesse.

Change is coming to higher education, make no mistake about that.
But it will likely be disruptive in ways different from what Christensen
and others have imagined. The growth in the overall size of the market for an undergraduate education has not benefited all institutions.

Most of the expansion in the market for a baccalaureate education has been soaked up by a limited number of big, prestigious, and rich institutions. Across the rest of the market, an embarrassingly high number of institutions have suffered enrollment declines of 10 percent or more. The smaller the institution, the more likely those declines threaten its sustainability and, in an increasing number of cases, make discussions of institutional closing both immediate and real. What the numbers tell us is that there is every reason to expect the next decade to bring more of the same as the rich get richer and the big get bigger.

The numbers also can help those who care about the nation's colleges and universities understand and prepare for a likely challenging future. The keeper of those numbers is the National Center for Education Statistics (NCES) and its principal depository, the Integrated Postsecondary Education Data System (IPEDS). IPEDS allows us to define the market for an undergraduate education in terms of principal sectors: Four-Year Public institutions, Four-Year Private Not-for-Profit institutions, Two-Year Public institutions, and Four-Year Private For-Profit institutions. While it is sometimes more satisfying to talk about a national market for postsecondary education—one that in 2016 collectively enrolled just over 15 million degree- and certificate-seeking undergraduates in the four sectors that are the focus of this study—it is more useful to talk about a host of separate and related markets loosely linked through rules the federal government uses to distribute student financial aid to qualifying students.

The numbers used in this study represent enrollments at undergraduate degree-granting and Title IV–eligible colleges and universities. We include both full- and part-time enrollments of undergraduates pursuing a degree or a certificate. (Occasionally, when IPEDS does not collect data for an important variable, such as ethnicity, for degree-/certificate-seeking students, we use instead the data reported for all enrolled undergraduates.) We further sharpened the focus of our analysis by restricting the data we extracted from IPEDS to a core list of institutions that are located in the 50 US states, and whose data consistency allows for multiyear analyses. Altogether 2,853 institutions from the market's four principal sectors met this standard: 552 Four-Year

Public institutions; 1,003 Four-Year Private Not-for-Profit institutions; 988 Two-Year Public institutions; and, from the analytically most problematic sector, 310 Four-Year Private For-Profit institutions. All told, the institutions in these four sectors reported enrolling 14,113,065 degree-/certificate-seeking undergraduates in 2016—a sum that represents 94 percent of the enrollments reported to IPEDS by all degree-granting Title IV institutions in the four sectors that are the subject of this volume. (For a more complete description of the inclusion rules we used to construct our database, see appendix B, "On Squaring the Circle.")

Still, drawing conclusions based on the numbers and their attendant graphs remains an interpretive adventure. We present two graphs, each using the same data that, nonetheless, yield quite different depictions of market shifts after 2008. The first plots how enrollments in each of the four sectors changed, in percentage terms, over time (figure 2.1). This graph suggests the kinds of disruptions that Christensen and others have frequently dwelled on. The Four-Year Private For-Profit sector is in near free fall, having erased all its dramatic gains in the 2008–2010 period and, in the process, closed upward of 200 sites. The Two-Year Public (community) colleges have suffered the same kind of losses—though it is important to point out that the trend for these institutions repeats the traditional pattern of rising and falling community college enrollments during, and then immediately following, a major

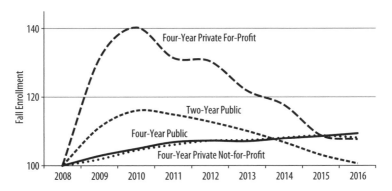

Figure 2.1. Fall enrollment of undergraduate degree-seeking students by sector 2008 to 2016. Indexed by setting 2008 values to 100.

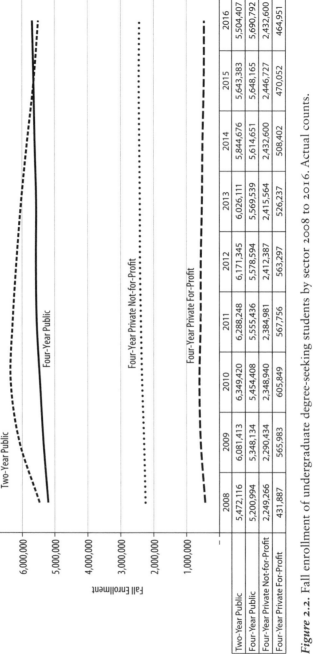

	2008	2009	2010	2011	2012	2013	2014	2015	2016
Two-Year Public	5,472,116	6,081,413	6,349,420	6,288,248	6,171,345	6,026,111	5,844,676	5,643,383	5,504,407
Four-Year Public	5,200,994	5,348,134	5,454,408	5,555,436	5,578,594	5,569,539	5,614,651	5,648,165	5,690,792
Four-Year Private Not-for-Profit	2,249,266	2,290,434	2,348,940	2,384,981	2,412,387	2,415,564	2,432,600	2,446,727	2,432,600
Four-Year Private For-Profit	431,887	565,983	605,849	567,756	563,297	526,237	508,402	470,052	464,951

Figure 2.2. Fall enrollment of undergraduate degree-seeking students by sector 2008 to 2016. Actual counts.

economic recession. The lines for the Four-Year Public and Four-Year Private Not-for-Profit providers are essentially identical and represent a steady expansion of the market.

Graphing the actual enrollments yields a different kind of picture, one in which there is neither great disruption nor substantial drama (figure 2.2). The Four-Year Private For-Profit sector largely fades from view. The relative stability of the markets for Four-Year Public and Four-Year Private Not-for-Profit colleges and universities becomes more apparent. The rise and fall of community college enrollments as the recession first deepened and then receded is properly scaled. The Four-Year Private For-Profit market is in steep decline, though the sector's role in either encouraging or discouraging college enrollments is clearly minimized. Thus, the dramatic changes that were purportedly taking place over this period do not, in fact, appear to have been terribly dramatic, at least in terms of enrollments in these sectors.

Shifts and Swirls

What the enrollment totals displayed in figure 2.2 hide, however, are the shifts and swirls that characterize competition for students within each of the four sectors. Among the three main groups of institutions highlighted—Four-Year Public institutions, Four-Year Private Not-for-Profit institutions, and Two-Year Public institutions—there have, in fact, been substantial enrollment losses, even though the markets in which they compete expanded. Nearly two-thirds of the Two-Year Public colleges lost enrollment; 47 percent of the Four-Year Private Not-for-Profit institutions did as well. In the Four-Year Public sector, whose colleges and universities could be said to have held their own, more than a third of those institutions were smaller in 2016 than they had been in 2008.

The winners and losers reflected in these market shifts are further highlighted when we disaggregate the sector data by geographic region, market segment, and institutional size. Being located in the Far West and Southwest was an advantage. Being big helped as well. However, the most market-defining attribute was market segment—or rank—as defined using the market taxonomy we presented in *The Market Imperative* (Zemsky and Shaman 2017). That study demonstrated that graduation rates were highly predictive of a set of attributes that included market price, student demographics, and *U.S. News & World Report* rankings. *The Market Imperative* described the five market segments as follows:

—*Medallion*: the segment comprising the nation's most competitive institutions and students; a segment for which prestige-based ranking plays a substantial role in defining institutional ambitions and quality.

—*Name Brand*: a segment largely populated by well-known institutions. Most practice selective admissions, though their appeal is more likely to be regional than national. Many but not all of these institutions would like to be Medallions.

—*Good Buy*: a segment comprising a variety of institutions, for the most part offering full-scale undergraduate programs at prices substantially less than those of higher-ranked institutions.

—*Good Opportunity*: a segment comprising institutions and students who see higher education as a special opportunity. Many students who shop in this segment are the first in their families to attend college.

—*Convenience*: the one segment in which part-time and intermittent learners dominate. Students in this segment often shop for a friendly environment at an institution that understands special needs, including the need to take courses at convenient times.

The Medallion and Name Brand segments were almost exclusively the preserve of the young. Institutions belonging to one of the remaining segments—Good Buy through Convenience—were characterized by having greater numbers of older as well as part-time students. At the same time, grouping the data by market segments yields a remarkably robust estimate of the actual cash or market price institutions charge. The higher the market rank, the higher the market price. What is most noticeable about the enrollment data arrayed in terms of market segments is that the result is frequently an ordered set—perfectly ordered in the case of the Four-Year Private Not-for-Profits. In the top portions of tables 2.1 and 2.2, the Four-Year Public and the Four-Year Private Not-for-Profit sector institutions at the top of the rankings—Medallion and Name Brand public institutions in the Public sector and Medallion institutions in the Private Not-for-Profit sector—were much less likely to have suffered 10 percent or greater enrollment losses following 2008. Conversely, those institutions at the bottom were much more likely to have suffered substantial enrollment losses. In other words, the most expensive institutions were least likely to lose enrollments, whereas those that charged the least lost the most enrollments over that period.

Remember market segment is defined in terms of graduation rate, which, in turn, is proxy for prestige and competitiveness. There are other attributes, which turn out to be related to segment, that make an independent contribution to an individual institution's market position.

Table 2.1. Enrollment shifts among Four-Year Public institutions, 2008–2016

	Institutions gaining enrollment	Institutions losing enrollment	% of institutions with enrollment losses ≥10%
Market segments			
Medallion	23	2	4
Name Brand	63	7	1
Good Buy	158	98	18
Good Opportunity	58	73	38
Convenience	30	21	27
Regions			
Far West	54	4	2
Rocky Mountains	17	11	14
Southwest	47	13	15
New England	20	21	22
Southeast	86	57	24
Plains	28	25	26
Mid-Atlantic	60	38	26
Great Lakes	31	40	31
2008 enrollment bands			
More than 25,000	28	4	6
20,001–25,000	29	10	13
15,001–20,000	40	10	12
10,001–15,000	49	20	14
5,001–10,000	89	64	20
1,501–5,000	72	77	33
1,500 or fewer	36	24	27

Table 2.2. Enrollment shifts among Four-Year Private Not-for-Profit institutions, 2008–2016

	Institutions gaining enrollment	Institutions losing enrollment	% of institutions with enrollment losses ≥10%
Market segments			
Medallion	92	26	2
Name Brand	76	72	22
Good Buy	159	164	32
Good Opportunity	145	136	35
Convenience	29	54	57
Regions			
Far West	71	30	17
New England	61	39	18
Rocky Mountains	10	5	20
Southwest	32	25	25
Southeast	140	96	27
Mid-Atlantic	96	99	29
Plains	51	67	35
Great Lakes	73	108	41
2008 enrollment bands			
More than 10,000	15	9	17
5,000–9,999	44	19	17
3,000–4,999	56	51	24
2,000–2,999	79	87	27
1,000–1,999	158	174	32
500–999	106	87	31
499 or fewer	76	42	31

Table 2.3. Enrollment shifts among Two-Year Public institutions, 2008–2016

	Institutions gaining enrollment	Institutions losing enrollment	% of institutions with enrollment losses ≥10%
Regions			
New England	23	22	22
Far West	70	103	32
Southwest	64	54	34
Plains	44	65	39
Rocky Mountains	16	22	39
Southeast	100	172	42
Mid-Atlantic	37	59	47
Great Lakes	31	106	62
2008 enrollment bands			
More than 25,000	9	9	28
15,001–25,000	19	38	35
7,501–15,000	59	90	34
3,501–7,500	116	141	33
1,501–3,500	94	200	51
751–1,500	46	85	52
750 or fewer	42	40	35

Table 2.4. Enrollment shifts among the market's three principal sectors

Sector	2016 (%)	2008 (%)	Shift (%)
Four-Year Public	42	40	2
Four-Year Private Not-for-Profit	18	17	1
Two-Year Public	40	42	−2

That becomes apparent when examining the data presented in tables 2.1 and 2.2.

In both tables 2.1 and 2.2, the winners were the big, top-ranked institutions. Conversely, being small, being located in the Mid-Atlantic, the Plains, or the Great Lakes, proved to be a disadvantage, as was being at or near the bottom of the market in terms of competitiveness. Table 2.3 presents a parallel summary for the community college market minus market segments. A large proportion of Two-Year Public institutions in the Great Lakes region, and to a lesser extent the Mid-Atlantic, experienced substantial losses. Again, small institutions—especially those with enrollments between 750 and 3,500—were subject to major declines.

Now take a look at table 2.4, which reflects the absence of major market shifts between sectors, reinforcing the conclusion that the dominant market shifts were within sectors.

First Findings

What should one take away from this initial analysis? Collectively, over the period 2008 to 2016, these data (figures 2.1, 2.2; tables 2.1–2.4) testify to an expanding, rather than a contracting, baccalaureate market. Whatever the changing supply of high school graduates, the number of enrolled students seeking an undergraduate education has increased over the past decade at a relatively constant rate. And though it has been an expanding market, it has also been one that has punished large numbers of institutions at the bottom. While the 9 percent increase in undergraduate enrollments of degree-/certificate-seeking students in both the Four-Year Public and the Four-Year Private Not-for-Profit sectors has been reassuring, what troubles the enterprise as a whole are the substantial number of colleges and universities that, nonetheless, suffered enrollment declines. Even institutions with only marginally smaller enrollments in 2016 than in 2008 were being left behind as the market expanded. Institutions experiencing 10 percent enrollment declines were already in trouble. And for the smaller set of institutions whose enrollments were diminished by 25 percent or more—all told, 12 percent of the Public Convenience segment and a whopping 39 percent of the Private Not-for-Profit Convenience segment—closing time has become a looming possibility.

The distribution of institutions with diminished enrollments is of particular interest here. In these analyses of the market for an undergraduate education in the United States, we have sliced and diced the market's principal sectors in terms of region, size of institution, and market segments—equally important categories when the task shifts to identifying which baccalaureate institutions are likely to face difficulties over the next decade. The details presented in tables 2.1–2.4 provide context for understanding what is likely to happen next. The focus should be on the "cut points"—what distinguished the institutions that grew and prospered from those that sustained significant losses?

Among the Four-Year Public colleges and universities, what mattered most was competitive muscle. In this sector, nearly 40 percent lost degree-/certificate-seeking undergraduates after 2008, while just over 20 percent experienced losses of 10 percent or more. But against that grim backdrop, only two institutions among those with market dominance—the 95 Medallion and Name Brand Public universities—had a 10 percent or greater enrollment decline, and only 9 had any loss of enrollment at all. For the sector's least competitive institutions, it proved a much rougher decade.

Size also mattered. The smaller the institution, the more likely it suffered enrollment losses greater than or equal to 10 percent from 2008 to 2016. The really big institutions—at least 25,000 degree-/certificate-seeking undergraduates—were largely immune. Just 2 out of the 32 universities in this category had enrollment losses of 10 percent or more. At the same time, more than half of the sector's biggest universities grew their enrollments by an additional 10 percent or more. Midsized universities (enrollments of degree-/certificate-seeking undergraduates of between 15,000 and 20,000) had roughly the same experience. While there were few institutions in this size range with substantial enrollment declines, it was also a group with just as few institutions with substantially larger enrollments. The losers were the smaller institutions—public baccalaureate colleges and universities with fewer than 5,000 degree-/certificate-seeking undergraduates. Collectively, more than a quarter of these institutions suffered enrollment losses of 10 percent or more.

Geographic region mattered, too. Western schools fared well; just one Far West Four-Year Public university had an enrollment loss greater than 10 percent, while 42 of the 58 institutions in California, Hawaii, Nevada, Oregon, and Washington experienced enrollment growth that exceeded 10 percent between 2008 and 2016. It was the institutions east of the Rockies that were in real trouble. On average, more than 25 percent of these institutions suffered enrollment declines of 10 percent or more.

The Four-Year Private Not-for-Profit sector exhibits many of the same characteristics in sharper relief, particularly when the focus is on market segments. Looking at the far-right column of table 2.1 ("% of Institutions with Enrollment Losses≥10%") notice how steeply the percentage of institutions increases as you move down the list from the most prestigious and market dominant to the least. Among the sector's Medallion institutions, only a handful experienced enrollment losses that exceeded 10 percent. Name Brand institutions were not as successful but still suffered fewer losses than the market in general. The bottom of the market was devastated—with more than half the Convenience institutions and a third of the Good Opportunity institutions, losing more than 10 percent of their degree-/certificate-seeking undergraduates.

Here institutional size has nearly the same impact as market segment, with most of the larger institutions holding their own, while smaller ones were struggling to maintain their degree-seeking undergraduate enrollment. The smaller the institution's undergraduate enrollment, the more likely it was to have a decline of 10 percent or more. Almost one in three colleges with fewer than 2,000 degree-/certificate-seeking undergraduates suffered enrollment declines exceeding 10 percent.

For these Four-Year Private Not-for-Profit institutions, the geography of loss replicated that of the Four-Year Public sector. The institutions in the Far West, Rocky Mountains, and Southwest—as well as New England—fared significantly better than those in the rest of the country. The losses across the Plains and Great Lakes were particularly grim, as well as noticeable.

The experience of the nation's Two-Year Public (community colleges) was even starker. As in the rest of the market, geography mattered. The biggest regional losers were community colleges across the Great Lakes region (Illinois, Indiana, Michigan, Wisconsin, and Ohio), where nearly three-quarters of the institutions had smaller undergraduate enrollments in 2016 than they had in 2008 and where more than 60 percent experienced enrollment losses greater than 10 percent.

Size of institution plays the same role in the community college market as it played in the baccalaureate market: the bigger the institution, the lower the probability of having smaller enrollments in 2016 than in 2008.

Tracking the Four-Year Private For-Profit sector is more difficult, largely because of the inconsistent data reported by the institutions. In all, we identified 310 Four-Year Private For-Profit institutions for which consistent data were available 2008 through 2016 from IPEDS. Collectively, they reported a total of 464,951 degree-/certificate-seeking undergraduate students in 2016, up from 431,887 undergraduates in 2008. These enrollment totals are also the beginning and endpoints of the graph in figure 2.2.

The Four-Year Private For-Profit sector matters less today than it did a decade ago. In our market database of Four-Year degree-granting institutions, the For-Profit sector accounts for just 5 percent of the total enrollments of degree-/certificate-seeking undergraduates. If the future can be predicted from the recent past for this relatively new sector of the industry, a continued downward spiral seems likely.

A Shifting Demographic

Often the predictions of declining enrollments and forced closures include a warning that the nation's colleges and universities are ill prepared for a pair of looming demographic changes. The first presages the emergence of adult learners as major higher education consumers along with the firms and businesses that employ them. From this perspective, college will no longer be exclusively for the young but, rather, a continuing experience that keeps rising generations of learners employment ready.

If past is prologue, however, the era of the adult learner is still a long way off. The fact of the matter is that college undergraduate populations have gotten both bigger and younger over the past decade—the proportion of undergraduates 25 years and older has actually declined everywhere. Only in the Four-Year Private For-Profit sector has the population being served gotten older and then by a considerable percentage (67% in 2015 vs. 57% in 2007). That the median institutional average of undergraduates 25 years or older is 64 percent is not surprising and indicates that the majority of Four-Year Private For-Profit institutions primarily serve adult learners (table 2.5).

Everywhere else that median percentage is not very different from what it was in 2007, particularly for Four-Year baccalaureate institutions, Public as well as Private Not-for-Profit. It is interesting to note that while the number of students 25 years and older has increased in these two sectors, their proportions on campuses have remained static or even have declined slightly over the last decade. Even when older

Table 2.5. Undergraduates 25 years and older

	2015 (N)	2015 (%)	2015 median institutional average (%)	2007 (N)	2007 (%)	2007 median institutional average (%)
Four-Year Public	983,796	17	17	974,391	18	17
Four-Year Private Not-for-Profit	547,431	21	12	474,611	21	15
Two-Year Public	2,410,910	35	33	2,580,850	40	39
Four-Year For-Profit	324,420	67	64	208,519	57	56

Table 2.6. Ethnicity of undergraduates, 2016 and 2010

	African American (%)	Hispanic (%)	Asian (%)	White (%)
Four-Year Public				
2016	11	15	7	56
2010	11	10	7	62
Four-Year Private Not-for-Profit				
2016	11	10	6	58
2010	12	7	5	61
Two-Year Public				
2016	14	25	6	45
2010	15	18	5	52
Four-Year Private For-Profit				
2016	24	15	3	43
2010	20	10	2	39

students have grown in number, their growth has been in the context of bigger increases in the younger student population. The nation's community colleges have, as before, continued to serve as centers of adult learners, though here, too, the enrollment numbers and median proportion of undergraduates 25 years or older have also declined.

Higher education's critics who focus on equity and inclusion were closer to the mark when they asked if higher education would be ready for a much more diverse student body—one that is decidedly less white. Table 2.6 presents the broad outlines of this shift and highlights the fact that the big increases were among Hispanic students, whose enrollments increased in all four sectors. Hispanic enrollments increased by just under 640,000 students, with 87 percent of that growth split almost evenly between the two Public sectors—Four-Year Public colleges and universities and Two-Year Public community colleges.

Three State Markets

Our analyses have, thus far, focused on the national data, acknowledging differences by geographic region. But, in many ways, a consideration of the market for higher education needs to acknowledge that what is true in one part of the nation is not equally true in every other

Table 2.7. Three state enrollment detail

	Four-Year Public	Four-Year Private Not-for-Profit	Two-Year Public	Total
Iowa				
2016 enrollment	63,157	37,773	52,513	153,443
Change from 2008	11,074	(3,623)	(10,127)	(2,676)
Institutions	3	26	16	45
Institutions losing enrollment	1	18	12	31
Institutions losing 10% or more	0	12	9	21
North Carolina				
2016 enrollment	177,001	66,247	177,909	420,714
Change from 2008	14,800	2,037	115	16,933
Institutions	16	36	59	111
Institutions losing enrollment	4	15	41	60
Institutions losing 10% or more	2	13	32	47
California				
2016 enrollment	630,273	153,912	1,282,203	2,066,388
Change from 2008	100,674	27,184	(93,324)	34,534
Institutions	32	66	110	208
Institutions losing enrollment	0	13	78	91
Institutions losing 10% or more	0	7	40	47

part. Those who work in those markets know better. Most students and their parents shop locally, most often choosing options that are just down the road or around the corner. What happens locally matters.

By way of illustration, we offer three examples of state markets where the competition among and between the sectors differs (table 2.7). Our first example is Iowa, a Plains state locked in the middle of the country where total undergraduate enrollments have collectively declined by just under 2 percentage points over the past decade. The experiences of individual institutions in Iowa, however, were starkly different. The state's 16 community colleges collectively lost 16 percent of their 2008 enrollments, 12 of these institutions had smaller enrollments in 2016 than in 2008, and 9 lost more that 10 percent of their 2008 enrollment of degree-/certificate-seeking undergraduates. In sharp contrast, Iowa's three Four-Year Public universities saw their collective undergraduate enrollments increase by 21 percent, but that summation is misleading. Within those three universities, the midmarket public comprehensive university lost nearly 10 percent of its 2008 enrollment, while the two public flagships increased their enrollments by 14 and 43 percent, respectively. The Four-Year Private Not-for-Profit sector, like the community college sector, lost enrollment—in all, enrollments in this sector of the market were down almost 9 percent. What many leaders of these Four-Year Private Not-for-Profit institutions concluded was that the public flagship with a 43 percent gain in enrollments of degree-/certificate-seeking undergraduates had, in fact, become a predator, spurred on by a Board of Regents determined to secure the future of Iowa's public universities at the expense of the state's private institutions and community colleges.

North Carolina presents a more balanced picture of the competition between the sectors. Here, as in Iowa, the big winners were the Four-Year Public universities, both flagships and comprehensives. The two best-known public universities mostly maintained their enrollments, while 6 of the lesser known comprehensives had enrollment growths exceeding 10 percent, and 2 had enrollment losses exceeding 10 percent. North Carolina's 59 community colleges held their own as well, though 41 of these institutions lost enrollments, while 32 suffered enrollment losses in excess of 10 percent. Just over a third of the private colleges and universities in the state suffered enrollment losses in excess of 10 percent.

California is the good news state. Overall, enrollments increased just slightly. But among the 32 Four-Year Public universities not one lost enrollment, and 25 of the 32—or more than 80 percent—reported enrollment gains in excess of 10 percent. The state's Two-Year Public institutions, like community colleges elsewhere, lost enrollment, but only modestly, about 7 percent. While almost 30 percent gained enrollment, 40 suffered enrollment losses in excess of 10 percent. Here, in contrast with Iowa and North Carolina, the Four-Year Private Not-for-Profit sector was the big winner: growing more than 21 percent since 2008 and limiting enrollment losses to just 7 of the 66 institutions in the sector. Given that student and family educational choices are constrained by the supply of local options, enrollment patterns within states provide crucial context for understanding an institution's future prospects.

Is There an Educational Desert?

Iowa and North Carolina are states with substantial rural populations. The new question being asked about rural America is whether the continued urbanization of the United States has made it more likely that rural students will be disadvantaged in their pursuit of a college education. The *New York Times* neatly summed up this concern noting that "approximately 11 million Americans live in 'education deserts' that are more than an hour's drive from a public college that accepts at least 30 percent of applicants. And millions more have sparse options, such as a single community college" (Chingos 2018).

Here the argument is about the options available to rural students, a perspective not reflected in the enrollment data we have been using thus far to describe the undergraduate market. The data again come from IPEDS, which used a 12-point scale to reflect the urbanization of the community in which each of the 2,800-plus colleges and universities that compose our core list of institutions are located. We reduced the IPEDS scale to just two measures, as follows: Institutions that are in communities that are cities (large, midsize, and small) or suburbs (large, midsize, and small) we labeled as being "more urban." Institutions that were located in communities that are towns (fringe, distant, and remote) or in communities that IPEDS identified as being rural (fringe, distant, and remote) we labeled as being "more rural."

We then compared the experiences of institutions in the two categories in terms of the proportion of enrollment achieved by each group and how often institutions in a given category suffered enrollment losses in excess of 10 percent since 2008.

Table 2.8 reflects the inequalities the *New York Times* was describing: enrollments in colleges and universities located in rural communities are less than 20 percent of the enrollments of institutions located in urban settings. At the same time, rural institutions experienced proportionally larger losses of students—except in the Four-Year Private Not-for-Profit sector, where the losses were more balanced between the more urban and more rural institutions. Given these distributions,

Table 2.8. Comparing urban and rural institutions' enrollment changes since 2008

	% of total enrollment in sector	% of institutions with enrollment losses ≥10%
Four-Year Public Colleges and Universities		
More urban	84	18
More rural	16	28
Four-Year Private Not-for-Profit Colleges and Universities		
More urban	84	28
More rural	16	31
Two-Year Public Colleges		
More urban	81	31
More rural	19	52

it is hard not to conclude that the rural educational desert that the *Times* worried about was often a function of the desire on the part of rural students to move to neighboring cities and suburbs.

A Market Hardly Imagined

While not everyone has joined Clayton Christensen in predicting a mass closing of institutions, there is, nonetheless, a growing sense that the enterprise may shortly face substantial numbers of institutional closings and forced mergers. We do not disagree, though our sense is that what is about to happen will be far less chaotic and less random than is imagined. In the coming chapters, we argue that what looms ahead is not an era of disruption but, rather, a time of consolidation that will likely be both painful and wasteful but not unexpected in either its consequences for students or its impacts on institutions.

Our argument stems from our understanding of the market—how it works, whom it advantages, and the nature of its constancy. We were struck again by how little the overall structure of the market has changed. The dominant segments have remained the same—what matters most, when it comes to predicting the cash or market price a given institution can expect its students to pay, is the institution's six-year graduation rate, which, not so surprisingly, tracks equally well with the institution's ranking by *U.S. News & World Report*. The market has not contracted in general, the two exceptions being the diminishing of the Four-Year Private For-Profit sector and the expected downturn in community college enrollment following the nation's recovery from an economic recession. Those who cite continuing shortfalls in college enrollments nationwide simply do not understand where their numbers are coming from.

What is most stunning about the market is how rigid it remains. The change that is present is predictable. The conclusion to remember—and the one that will shape our understanding of which institutions face the greatest market stress—is simply that the rich are getting richer, the big are getting bigger, and geography matters. Everyone else is scrambling. Recall the distribution of institutions that suffered enrollment losses in excess of 10 percent after 2008. Among Four-Year Public universities, a third or more of the institutions in the bottom two market segments lost 10 percent or more of their degree/certificate undergraduate enrollments. Among Four-Year Private Not-for-Profit institutions, a third or more, in all three bottom market segments (Good Buy, Good Opportunity, Convenience), lost 10 percent or more of their enrollment. In this sector only, the Medallion institutions remained unscathed. A second tell-tale sign was having fewer than 1,500 enrolled undergraduates. The third important predictor was region: while the Far West and Southwest regions grew in enrollments, institutions in the Plains and Great Lakes were being hollowed out.

The importance of these predictors should not be underestimated. They tell institutional leaders two things. First, the market is squeezing them; they may well have done nothing wrong. Second, it is important for each institution to understand the specific attributes that define their market stress. It is the task of providing a practical metric for the stress analysis that we turn to next.

THREE

A Calculus for Risk

ERE'S THE QUESTION we often hear: Why bother to estimate an individual institution's risk of closing? When the news is bad enough, everybody knows the institution faces an impending crisis. Programs have been closed or neglected; enrollments have declined; a hiring freeze has been imposed—all of which lead inevitably to a campus permeated with a mood of pessimism. While all of that is true of institutions on the brink of collapse, what of those institutions that are not yet in such dire straits? How is an institution to monitor its fitness so that it can head off serious trouble—or plan for the inevitable? Our answer is that a well-constructed risk score quantifying institutional viability can productively reshape the discussion of institutional futures, making them more purposeful and less emotive. And that is precisely what campus leaders, along with those responsible for the public policies that impact higher education, need to have happen before, rather than after, they seek corrective actions.

In chapter 1, we described the three basic languages most often used to discuss college closings: a *language of threat*, a *language of reassurance*, and a *language of grief*. Our risk analysis employs a fourth language, one that most often is used to predict weather events. In our language of market stress there are *alerts* (akin to "watches" in a weather forecast) and *warnings*. The models of the National Weather

Service combine measures, including those that track changes in barometric pressure, wind speed, and temperature, to assess the risk of serious storms and to form the basis for the Weather Service's storm watches and warnings. In a parallel fashion, our Market Stress Test Scores, both graphically and arithmetically, track changes in a key set of market components that form the basis for issuing alerts and warnings.

Moving forward in this chapter we describe the variables—or components—used in the computation of risk scores that comprise the Market Stress Test Score. Then we go on to describe the methodology used to determine the scores. Since some of the components differ across sectors, a separate section of this chapter is devoted to each sector.

The Market Stress Test Score is a composite of multiple market components, each reflecting a separate aspect of the change in an institution's market position over a period of eight years, usually 2008 through 2016. Each component satisfies two additional criteria. It must derive from institutional data available from IPEDS for nearly all accredited institutions regularly and consistently reporting enrollment and related data to the federal government, and the correlation between any two components must be negligible. The factors included in the calculation of our Market Stress Test Score should surprise no one. They relate to stable and sustained enrollments, secure revenue streams, and reasonable expenditures.

For Four-Year Private Not-for-Profit Colleges and Universities

For the Four-Year Private Not-for-Profit sector, the components that comprise the Market Stress Test Score fall into two broad categories: enrollment and financial. Enrollment health is gauged by an institution's ability to each year matriculate first-year degree-seeking undergraduates—here also labeled "first-year" or "freshman"—and the institution's power to retain those students the next year. For first-year enrollment, the key measures tracked by the Market Stress Test Score are the magnitude of the percentage change in the numbers of freshmen

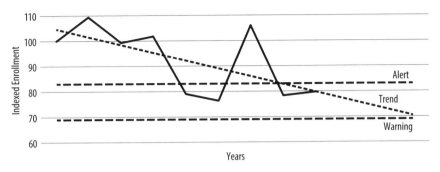

Figure 3.1. First-year enrollment at a midwestern liberal arts college. Indexed by setting 2008 values to 100.

between 2008 and 2016 (the last year for which IPEDS data are available for our analysis) and the slope of the trend line—that is, the linear fit of the annual percentage change in the number of new first-year students. These measures are compared to alert and warning thresholds. Figure 3.1 illustrates the changes in first-year enrollment for a midwestern liberal arts college facing tough sledding in an increasingly competitive market. While reading the graph in figure 3.1, note that the actual enrollment numbers are indexed relative to the 2008 data so that the percentage change is easily discerned. Observe, then, that the fall 2016 enrollment is at 80, indicating that the latest first-year enrollment is only 80 percent of freshman enrollment in 2008, or a 20 percent decline from the initial fall 2008 number. Determination of the alert and warning values shown in figure 3.1 will be discussed in detail later in this chapter.

The other enrollment component, first-year to second-year retention, is computed by determining how many students in the first-year full-time cohort return to campus the following year. Here the useful values are both the actual retention rate in fall 2016 and the slope of the trend line reflecting change over time from 2008 to 2016. Figure 3.2 graphs the results for the same institution presented in figure 3.1. In this case, freshman-to-sophomore retention is stable and above the alert line.

The two financial measures, market price and the ratio of endowment to expense, measure income stability and control of expenses:

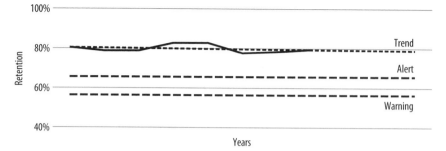

Figure 3.2. First-year retention at a midwestern liberal arts college.

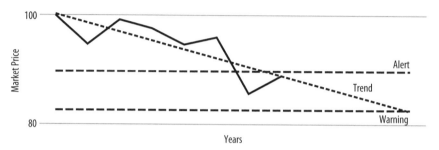

Figure 3.3. Market price of a midwestern liberal arts college 2008 to 2015. Indexed by setting 2008 values to 100.

market price is the flip side of tuition discount. The market price reflects the average tuition and fees the institution receives after the average discount in the form of institutional financial aid has been applied. The change in market price from 2008 to 2015—cast in constant 2008 dollars in this analysis—reflects a change in the stated tuition and fees, a change in the amount of institutional aid expended, or both.

In figure 3.3, the slope of the trend line is negative because the institutional aid (discounts) this liberal arts college awarded enrolling students increased faster than its sticker price. In this example, both the percentage change over the period and the trend line of the constant dollar market price end below the alert line.

For a large proportion of institutions in this sector, a declining market price reflects an institution's struggle to recruit a new class and the heightened competition it is experiencing. IPEDS limits the information about institutionally funded financial aid—the tuition discount—

to moneys allocated for full-time first-year students. The market price is the average discounted tuition price for just that set of students. Changes in market price thus become a reasonable proxy for the way in which overall net undergraduate tuition income is changing.

The second financial measure is a ratio of the endowment to total expenses. There is little written by either economists or experts in philanthropy about what the optimal size of an endowment should be relative to an institution's expense budget. Much is written instead about spending rates, investment plans, and sustainability of funding for programs. Fund-raisers often allow that a healthy ratio results when the endowment is two to three times the size of annual expenses. For Tony Poderis, former director of development for the Cleveland Orchestra,

> the formidable objective of having an endowment fund in an amount three times (or any number) that of the annual operating budget, or any attempt to set a standard, or even a benchmark, must be considered with many other factors. . . . So, how much endowment should/must we have in hand anyway? Simply put; as much as you can raise with an effort that in no way will interfere with, slow down, or be a substitute for the best annual fund campaign you can mount—year after year. (Poderis 2019)

With that in mind, the score for this financial component is not based on the absolute endowment-to-expense ratio but, rather, is computed using the change from 2008 to 2015 in the ratio of the end-of-year endowment value to that same year's total expenses (omitting hospitals when universities have associated hospitals). A downturn in that ratio may be driven by a decline in the endowment value, an increase in expenses, or, as is often the case, both simultaneously. In figure 3.4, the overall trend line is positive, and the 2015 ratio is above the alert line, albeit moving down for the past few years.

For Four-Year Public Institutions

Four-Year Public colleges and universities share many of the same risk elements as their Private Not-for-Profit counterparts. Again, the Market

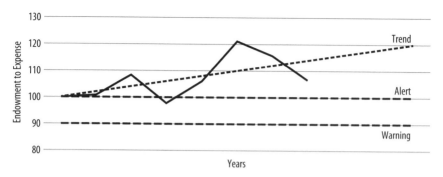

Figure 3.4. Endowment-to-expense ratio at a midwestern liberal arts college 2008 to 2015. Indexed by setting 2008 values to 100.

Stress Test Score comprises two enrollment and two financial components. Like private institutions public institutions are heavily dependent on the new enrollment and retention of new students, so those measures contribute to the Market Stress Test Scores for public institutions. Despite posting price tags considerably lower than those of most private institutions, public institutions engage in discounting to boost enrollment. Change in market price over time along with the slope of the fitted line reflecting the trajectory of the change in institutions' cash or discounted tuition income constitute the third component of the Market Stress Test Scores for Four-Year Public institutions. As in the analysis of the market prices set by Four-Year Private Not-for-Profit institutions, a deflator is applied to present all values in 2008 dollars.

Computing market price for public institutions is a bit more complicated than computing for private institutions. In the public sector, the differences in tuition and fees for in-state and out-of-state students must be considered. Fortunately, IPEDS makes available published tuition and fees for both in-state and out-of-state enrollees and provides a profile of residency of undergraduates by state. The latter allows for the calculation of an average tuition rate by applying the proportion of students paying in-state tuition and those paying out-of-state tuition.

The fourth Market Stress Test Score component for Four-Year Public institutions is different. Most Four-Year Public institutions in our data set have endowments, and it is possible to construct an endowment-to-expense ratio. Some of the endowments, for example, the Universi-

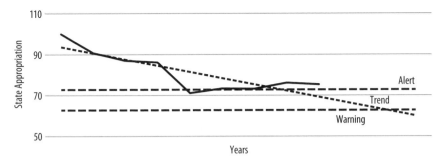

Figure 3.5. State appropriation for a public regional comprehensive university 2008 to 2016. Indexed by setting 2008 values to 100.

ties of Texas, Michigan, and Virginia, rival those of the richest private institutions. However, the endowments at most public colleges and universities are on average considerably smaller contributors to the bottom line than those in the Four-Year Private Not-for-Profit sector, and income derived from them plays a less important role in protecting the fiscal health of an institution.

Instead, in the Market Stress Test Score analysis, the key income factor for public institutions is the state appropriation. For at least half of the institutions in our data set, state appropriations in 2015–2016 covered more than a quarter of an institution's expenses. The value computed for the appropriation component is based on the change in the appropriation, in constant 2008 dollars, between 2008 and 2016. Figure 3.5 graphs the public appropriations received by a public regional comprehensive university.

What is most evident is the downward slope of the trend line, though, in this state, the end of the recession signaled an end of further reductions in state funding that four years later was followed by a very modest increase.

For Two-Year Public Institutions

Compared to Four-Year Public and Not-for-Profit institutions, Two-Year Public colleges operate on a very different model. Many of their programs are short—often a year or less in length. At the same time, students may stretch out the two-year associate degree programs over many years by attending part-time or intermittently. Two-Year institutions are highly dependent on two sources of income: tuition and public funding. While over two-thirds of the Two-Year colleges whose data are included in this study have endowment funds, they are, on average, small and represent more than one year's expenses in only three of the 988 institutions in the relevant data set. In contrast tuition accounts for nearly 60 percent of total revenue in at least half of the colleges, and state and local appropriations cover more than 40 percent of total expenses, on average.

Three components were used to form the Market Stress Test Score for the Two-Year Public sector, one measuring enrollment and two tracking financial data. The enrollment factor is the change in the number of entering students. Unlike the metric for Four-Year institutions, these counts are not restricted to students who are enrolled in a degree program.

Institutional discounting is not as pervasive or important across the Two-Year Public sector as it is in the Four-Year sectors. The median discount rate among community colleges and similarly configured institutions was calculated by taking institutional financial aid as a percentage of tuition income. At Two-Year Public institutions, the average discount rate for first-time full-time undergraduates is around 3 percent, compared with more than 20 percent for the same group of students at Four-Year Public institutions. Instead of market price, then, we measure tuition income as a share of instructional costs. Tuition represents the largest part of most two-year colleges' total income, while instructional costs account for upward of 42 percent of expenses on average. Changes in the ratio of tuition to instruction reflect a number of changes—enrollments and tuition rates on the one hand and class sizes, course offerings, faculty deployment, full versus part-time instructors, average faculty salary on the other (figure 3.6).

Finally, as is the case in the Four-Year Public sector, the Two-Year Public sector is heavily dependent on government appropriations. Because many community colleges and other Two-Year institutions receive substantial funding from their local municipalities, townships,

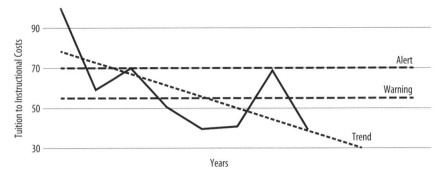

Figure 3.6. Ratio of tuition income to instructional costs at a Two-Year Public college. Indexed by setting 2008 values to 100.

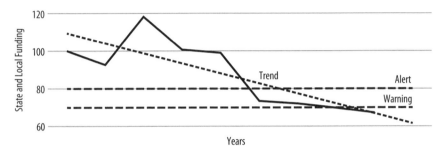

Figure 3.7. State and local funding for a community college on the decline. 2008–2015. Indexed by setting 2008 values to 100.

or counties, both state and local support are included. The federal government also appropriates funds to a small number of Two-Year institutions—fewer than 3 percent of the colleges in our data set. These federal dollars are not included in the computation. The community college whose state and local funding is presented in figure 3.7 is in considerable trouble. Its funding from these sources is on a persistent downward slope, and, in the analysis, the latest year of public funding fell below the warning line.

Constructing a Market Stress Test Score

The individual components of a Market Stress Test Score reflect two related criteria. The first, change over time, involves developing alert and warning points, or thresholds, and comparing the percentage change in each component over the period under study to each of those two values. For example, the percentage change in the number of first-time degree-seeking undergraduates, between an initial year, 2008, and the most recent year in the analysis set, 2016, is compared to an established alert value and warning value. Similarly, for the student retention component, the actual retention rate in the latest available year is tested against alert and warning values. The second criterion, "negative trend," asks if the value of the component is declining and on a trajectory that predicts a drop in the percentage change to or below the alert mark in the future.

The thresholds, or boundary points, are then determined by examining the distribution of each component's value, for example, the percent change in market price from 2008 to 2015, within each sector for all the institutions in the data set. The alert threshold is set at the 20th percentile of the distribution of the component in question; the warning boundary is the value at the lowest 10th percentile. For example, among Four-Year Public colleges and universities the 20th percentile for the percent change from 2008 to 2016 in the number of first-year degree-seeking undergraduates falls just below −15 percent, while at the 10th percentile the change falls just below −25 percent. Put another way, 20 percent of the Four-Year Public institutions in our set saw a more than 15 percent decline in new freshmen between fall 2008 and fall 2016 (namely, first-timers dropped to less than 85% of their 2008 value by 2016); thus, those institutions crossed the alert line. Ten percent crossed the warning threshold, with the fall 2016 freshmen enrollment falling to under 75 percent of the number in 2008; that is, they experienced a more than 25 percent decline in freshmen over that same period. The score is constructed by assigning one point for a change over time at or below the alert threshold and an additional point if that change reaches or crosses below the warning threshold.

The second criterion, "negative trend," asks whether the component shows decline over time such that it is likely to cross the alert boundary by 2019. For example, for each institution in the Four-Year Private Not-for-Profit sector, does the market price have a negative trajectory based on fitting a straight line to the yearly data, and does that line reach the alert boundary? Using the percent change in annual numbers of incoming new students for each college in the Two-Year Public set, is the slope of the straight line negative, and does it breach the alert threshold? If the answer is yes, then that component is given a score of 1.

All told, each college and university can receive a risk score for a given factor ranging from 0 to 3. An institution receives a 0 for a particular component if (1) the change over time (or for retention, the rate) *does not* reach the alert line and (2) the trend line of the data *does not* have a negative slope that is projected to reach the alert line. (Figure 3.2 displays an example of a component that has a zero score.) By contrast, an institution receives a 3 if (1) the negative trend reaches the alert line, (2) the "change over time" both falls below the alert line and (3) reaches or falls below the warning line. (Figure 3.7 provides an example of a factor that receives a score of 3.) Risk scores of 1 or 2 are achieved if some but not all of the criteria are met. (For example, a score of 2 is assigned to the component in figure 3.3.) Since four components are assessed for the Four-Year sectors and three are assessed for the Two-Year sector, an institution's total Market Stress Test Score can range from 0 to 12 in the first case, or 0 to 9 in the second.

Table 3.1 provides a schematic summarizing how Market Stress Test Scores are assigned. Tables 3.2 to 3.4 display the specific scoring criteria

Table 3.1. General schematic for calculating Market Stress Test Scores

	Criteria		
Score components	Component reaches or crosses below the alert line[a]	Component reaches or crosses below the warning line[b]	Trend is negative– projected to reach or cross alert line by 2019
1	Add 1	Add 1	Add 1
2	Add 1	Add 1	Add 1
3	Add 1	Add 1	Add 1
4 Four-Year institutions only	Add 1	Add 1	Add 1

[a] Twentieth percentile among all institutions in data set.
[b] Tenth percentile among all institutions in data set.

Table 3.2. Four-Year Private Not-for-Profit scoring schematic

Score component	Criteria		
	Component reaches or crosses below the alert line (20th percentile among all institutions in data set)	Component reaches or crosses below the warning line (10th percentile among all institutions in data set)	Trend is negative– projected to reach or cross alert line by 2019
First year: % change in the number of first-time degree-seeking undergraduates (fall 2008–fall 2016)	Alert threshold, −17.3% Component at or below the threshold, +1 Otherwise, 0	Warning threshold, −30.6% Component at or below the threshold, +1 Otherwise, 0	Meets the criteria, +1 Otherwise, 0
Retention: percentage of full-time first-time cohort who enroll the following year (2007 to 2008 through 2015 to 2016)	Alert threshold, 65.6% Component at or below the threshold, +1 Otherwise, 0	Warning threshold, 56.4% Component at or below the threshold, +1 Otherwise, 0	Meets the criteria, +1 Otherwise, 0
Market price: % change in the average first-year full-time tuition minus institutional financial aid in constant dollars (2008–2015)[a]	Alert threshold, −10.4% Component at or below the threshold, +1 Otherwise, 0	Warning threshold, −17.5% Component at or below the threshold, +1 Otherwise, 0	Meets the criteria, +1 Otherwise, 0
Endowment to expense: % change in the ratio of the year-end value of the endowment to that year's expense (2008–2009 to 2015–2016)	Alert threshold, 0%[a] Component at or below the threshold, +1 Otherwise, 0	Warning threshold, −10.3% Component at or below the threshold, +1 Otherwise, 0	Meets the criteria, +1 Otherwise, 0

[a] This value is at the 18.5th percentile, where the first nonnegative value is found.

for institutions in each of the three sectors in the analysis. Each figure summarizes the definitions of the components discussed earlier and displays the criteria for reaching or crossing the alert and then the warning thresholds.

In Tables 3.2–3.4, all the criteria at the 10th percentile are negative—in many cases extremely negative. At the 20th percentile, nearly all the criteria are negative. However, in two instances, endowment to expense for Private Not-for-Profits, and market price in constant dollars for Four-Year Public institutions, the 20th percentile yields cut points that are slightly positive. Since it is not sensible to award a risk point to an institution whose overall change in a particular component is positive, albeit only slightly so, the threshold is adjusted to

Table 3.3. Four-Year Public scoring schematic

Score component	Criteria		
	Component reaches or crosses below the alert line (20th percentile among all institutions in data set)	Component reaches or crosses below the warning line (10th percentile among all institutions in data set)	Trend is negative– projected to reach or cross alert line by 2019
First year: % change in the number of first-time degree-seeking undergraduates (fall 2008–fall 2016)	Alert threshold, –15.4% Component at or below the threshold, +1 Otherwise, 0	Warning threshold, –25.6% Component at or below the threshold, +1 Otherwise, 0	Meets the criteria, +1 Otherwise, 0
Retention: percentage of full-time first-time cohort who enroll the following year (2007 to 2008 through 2015 to 2016)	Alert threshold, 67.8.% Component at or below the threshold, +1 Otherwise, 0	Warning threshold, 61.9% Component at or below the threshold, +1 Otherwise, 0	Meets the criteria, +1 Otherwise, 0
Market price: % change in the average first-year full-time tuition minus institutional financial aid in constant dollars (2008–2015)[a]	Alert threshold, 0%[a] Component at or below the threshold, +1 Otherwise, 0	Warning threshold, –8.3% Component at or below the threshold, +1 Otherwise, 0	Meets the criteria, +1 Otherwise, 0
Appropriation: change in the state appropriation in constant dollars (2007–2008 to 2015–2016)	Alert threshold –27.2% Component at or below the threshold, +1 Otherwise, 0	Warning threshold, –37.2% Component at or below the threshold, +1 Otherwise, 0	Meets the criteria, +1 Otherwise, 0

[a] This value is at the 18.5th percentile, where the first nonnegative value is found.

zero—no growth. Zero falls at around the 18th percentile in both cases.

The threshold values not only represent the bottom of the distribution for each component but also represent the values that hold up to a reasonableness test. Tables 3.2 and 3.3, in particular, show that the 20th and 10th percentiles produce threshold criteria for enrollments that are prima facie reasonable. Unless purposely planned (a rarity), a drop in the number of freshmen by 17 percent over eight years for Four-Year Private Not-for-Profit in the first case or 15 percent in Four-Year Public in the second, is cause for concern for most admissions offices. Similarly, a 30 or 25 percent drop in first-timers, respectively, represents a serious problem. Retention rates south of 70 percent are undesirable, and rates close to or less than 60 percent may cause severe difficulties for sustaining the size of the student body.

Table 3.4. Two-Year Public scoring schematic

| | Criteria | | |
Score component	Component reaches or crosses below the alert line (20th percentile among all institutions in data set)	Component reaches or crosses below the warning line (10th percentile among all institutions in data set)	Trend is negative–projected to reach or cross alert line by 2019
New students: % change in the number of first-time students (fall 2008–fall 2016)	Alert threshold, −29.2% Component at or below the threshold, +1 Otherwise, 0	Warning threshold, −42.4% Component at or below the threshold, +1 Otherwise, 0	Meets the criteria, +1 Otherwise, 0
Tuition revenue to instructional costs: % change in the ratio of tuition and fee income minus discounts to instructional costs (2007–2008 to 2015–2016)	Alert threshold, −28.3% Component at or below the threshold, +1 Otherwise, 0	Warning threshold, −38.4% Component at or below the threshold, +1 Otherwise, 0	Meets the criteria, +1 Otherwise, 0
Appropriations: % change in the state and local appropriations in constant dollars (2007–2008 to 2015–2016)	Alert threshold, −19.8% Component at or below the threshold, +1 Otherwise, 0	Warning threshold, −27.9% Component at or below the threshold, +1 Otherwise, 0	Meets the criteria, +1 Otherwise, 0

On the financial side, large falloffs in government appropriations spell major trouble for Two- and Four-Year Public institutions. A decline in appropriated funds in constant dollars of nearly 28 percent is problematic for Two-Year Public colleges (the warning threshold), and for Four-Year Publics, losing more than 37 percent of their real-dollar appropriations is assumed to cause major disruptions. Four-Year Private Not-for-Profits whose market price in constant dollars drops by more than 10 percent are jeopardizing their cash flow, and a larger risk ensues if the price drop exceeds 17.5 percent.

Although a Market Stress Test Score is computed for every institution in our data set, some institutions are missing the IPEDS records needed to evaluate one or more components, rendering their Market Stress Test Score invalid for the purposes of our analyses. For that reason, we limit the discussions in this and later chapters to those institutions with a score for every component. In the Four-Year Private Not-for-Profit sector 900 of the 1,003 colleges and universities in the data set—or just under 90 percent—are included. Of the 552 institutions in the Four-Year Public data set, 490, again, nearly 90 percent, have requisite data for all four components. Finally, nearly 95 percent, 930 of 988, of the Two-Year Public institutions in our data set have scores for all three components.

To illustrate the Market Stress Test Score construction, three examples are provided, one with a relatively high score, one with a problematic but more modest score, and one with a low score (tables 3.5–3.7). The first institution is a small private liberal arts college (Four-Year Private Not-for-Profit) located in the western part of the United States (table 3.5). This institution is experiencing enrollment issues with declining numbers of first-year full-time students and a retention rate

Table 3.5. High Market Stress Test Score example (Four-Year Private Not-for-Profit small liberal arts college)

	Score component			
	First year: % change in the number of first-time degree-seeking undergraduates (fall 2008–fall 2016)	*Retention:* percentage of full-time first-time cohort who enroll the following year (2015–2016)	*Market price:* % change in the average first year full-time tuition minus institutional financial aid in constant dollars (2008–2015)	*Endowment to expense:* % change in the ratio of the year-end value of the endowment to that year's total expenses (2008–2009 to 2015–2016)
Alert/warning thresholds (%)	−17.3/−30.6	65.6/56.4	−10.4/−17.5	0/−10.3
Change over time, or rate (%)	−17.5	64.8	−19.2	16.3
Projected change by 2019 (%)	−17.9	73.3	−26.5	36.2
Slope of trend line	−0.16	1.2%	−2.59	3.25%
Market Stress Test components				
Change over time, or rate reaches alert threshold	1	1	1	0
Change over time, or rate reaches warning threshold	0	0	1	0
Slope is negative/ projected to cross alert line	1	0	1	0
Component risk score	2	1	3	0
Market Stress Test Score	6			

Table 3.6. Problematic Market Stress Test Score example (Midwest public flagship)

	Score component			
	First year: % change in the number of first-time degree-seeking undergraduates (fall 2008–fall 2016)	*Retention:* percentage of full-time first-time cohort who enroll the following year (2015 to 2016)	*Market price:* % change in the average first-year full-time tuition minus institutional financial aid in constant dollars (2008–2015)	*Appropriation:* % change in the state appropriation in constant dollars (2007–2008 to 2015–2016)
Alert/warning thresholds (%)	−15.4/−25.6	67.8/61.9	0/−8.3	−27/37.2
Institutional values				
Change over time, or rate (%)	−12.6	62.4	18.4	−23.9
Projected change by 2019	−19.0	60.7	28.9	−38.2
Slope of trend line	−19.3	−0.2%	2.2%	−3.6
Market Stress Test Score components				
Change over time, or rate reaches alert threshold	0	1	0	0
Change over time, or rate reaches warning threshold	0	0	0	0
Slope is negative/ projected to cross alert line	1	1	0	1
Component risk score	1	2	0	1
Market Stress Test Score	4			

that is holding its own but is in a precarious range. The considerable market price drop combined with enrollment problems puts this institution at risk.

The second example is a campus in a midwestern state system (table 3.6). The change in its first-year enrollment is negative but above the alert threshold. However, the trend line fitted to the data projects a drop below the alert line by 2019. The more serious problem is student retention, which is just above the warning boundary and on a negative trajectory. Finally, the drop in the state appropriation is troubling. While it is not in the lowest 20 percent (alert boundary) among the Four-Year Public institutions in our data set, it is nevertheless predicted to fall below that mark by 2019.

Table 3.7. Minimal Market Stress Test Score example (southeastern community college)

	Score component		
	New students: % change in the number of first-time students (fall 2008–fall 2016)	*Tuition income to instructional costs:* % change in the ratio of tuition and fee income minus discounts to instructional costs (2007–2008 to 2015–2016)	*Appropriations:* % change in the state and local appropriations in constant dollars, 2007–2008 to 2015–2016
Alert/warning thresholds (%)	−29.2/−42.4	−28.3 /−38.4	−19.8/−27.9
Institutional values			
Change over time (%)	36.2	−11.2	3.5
Projected change by 2019 (%)	49.8	1.8	−5.1[a]
Slope of trend line	4.1	0.8	0.65
Market Stress Test Score components			
Change over time, or slope reaches alert threshold	0	0	0
Change over time, or slope reaches warning threshold	0	0	0
Slope is negative/projected to cross alert line	0	0	0
Component risk score			
Market Stress Test Score	0		

[a]While the slope is positive, funding drops from 2010 to 2013 caused the trend line to begin below the 2008 value, which resulted in a projected 2019 value below that of 2008.

Table 3.8. Distribution of institutions by Market Stress Test Scores

Market Stress Test Score	Public Four-Year	Private Four-Year Not-for-Profit	Public Two-Year
0	142	323	244
1	91	132	201
2	65	137	160
3	79	149	176
4	43	50	75
5	35	54	45
6	14	28	24
7	8	8	3
8	8	12	2
9	4	7	0
10	0	0	0
11	0	0	0
12	1	0	0
Total with scores	490	900	930

Finally, the Two-Year Public community college located in the Southeast (table 3.7) is doing well according to our risk analysis. All but one of its risk components are positive, and the one negative, the change in tuition to instructional costs, is at the 35th percentile among the peer institutions, well above the alert criterion.

The Landscape of Institutional Market Stress

As was noted earlier, Market Stress Test Scores run the gamut from a low of 0 to as high as 12 for four-year institutions, and 0 to 9 for two-year colleges. In reality, far fewer institutions score at the high end, 4 or more, than at the low end, 0 or 1—that is, few institutions are in extreme negative territory for multiple components. That said, the numbers of institutions that show substantial risk of 4 or greater is not trivial. Table 3.8 shows the distribution of risk scores among institutions in the three sectors in the study. Nearly half of the Four-Year Public colleges and universities have risk scores of 0 or 1—minimal risk, while less than one-quarter are in the substantial risk zone with scores of 4 to 12. The figure for those at minimal risk in the Four-Year Private Not-for-Profit sector is just over 50 percent compared with 18 percent scoring 4 or higher. Similarly, nearly half of the Two-Year Public colleges post scores in the minimal risk area, while 16 percent receive an index of 4 or more out of a possible nine.

With these figures in mind, the next chapter moves forward to examine the characteristics of those institutions at minimal, moderate, and substantial risk. After that, the characteristics of the students who attend institutions in the various risk categories are investigated to flesh out which populations are most vulnerable as institutions begin to experience problems.

FOUR

The Distribution of Risk

A DESCRIPTION OF MARKET risk across the higher education land-scape is now possible. In all, we have Market Stress Test Scores for just over 2,300 individual colleges and universities: 490 Four-Year Public institutions, 900 Four-Year Private Not-for-Profit institutions, and 930 Two-Year Public institutions. Missing are stress scores for Four-Year Private For-Profit institutions, the most disrupted portion of the market. In this sector, substantial enrollment increases during the height of the 2007–2011 financial crisis were followed by nearly as dramatic enrollment contractions. Amid the closings and consoli-dations that came to characterize the for-profit sector were major contractions by three of the biggest names in the industry: the University of Phoenix, DeVry University, and Kaplan University. At the same time, it was the for-profit sector that had the largest number of in-complete as well as missing and inconsistent IPEDS filings. What are available are consistent enrollment reports for 313 for-profit institu-tions, 54 percent of which reported enrollment declines of 25 percent or more after 2008.

There are two views for understanding market risk. The first fo-cuses on how many students in the market's three principal sectors were enrolled in institutions facing minimal, moderate, or substantial risk in 2016. The second summarizes how many institutions in each sector face minimal, moderate, or substantial risk.

A Student Distribution of Risk

The answers provided by the first metric are the easiest to summarize. All told, the 2,320 institutions for which it was possible to calculate a Market Stress Test Score in 2016 enrolled 13,016,205 undergraduates—41 percent in Two-Year Public institutions, 42 percent in Four-Year Public institutions, and 17 percent in Four-Year Private Not-for-Profit institutions. Most of those students (57%) attended institutions facing minimal risk; roughly a third (31%) attended institutions scored as experiencing moderate risk; and only 12 percent attended two- or four-year institutions facing substantial risk. Fewer than 7 percent attended four-year institutions at the highest levels of substantial risk, that is, with risk scores at or above 6. That so comparatively few students were in this latter category helps bolster the conclusion that the years ahead are not likely to see many students displaced as a result of institutional closings.

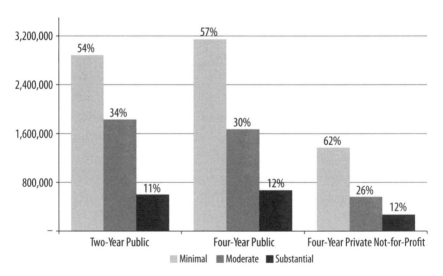

Figure 4.1. Distribution of undergraduate enrollment in 2016 by sector and risk category based on Market Stress Test Scores.

Figure 4.1 depicts the distribution of students in each sector in terms of the degree of risk faced by the institution they were attending in 2016. The most striking aspect of this display is just how similar the distributions are.

The Four-Year Public Market

The other metric depicting the distribution of risk focuses not on students but on the institutions they attended. The Market Stress Test Scores for the 2,300-plus institutions yield a host of interesting findings, starting with the Four-Year Public colleges and universities that represent the most stable part of the market.

The detailed distribution of Market Stress Test Scores becomes more interesting when the sector results are disaggregated first by region and then by institutional size and market segment—each attribute plays an important role in determining the volume of at-risk institutions. Geographically, the distribution of risk bears a striking resemblance to the nation's politics. The institutions least at risk are in the Far West, the Mid-Atlantic, and New England, and those most at risk are in the Great Lakes and the south (figure 4.2). It is a pattern that largely reflects the net impact of reductions in state funding for Four-Year Public colleges and universities.

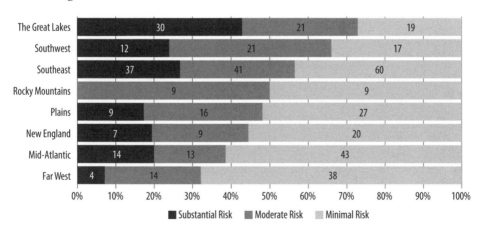

Figure 4.2. Number and percentage of Four-Year Public institutions in three risk categories based on Market Stress Test Scores by region.

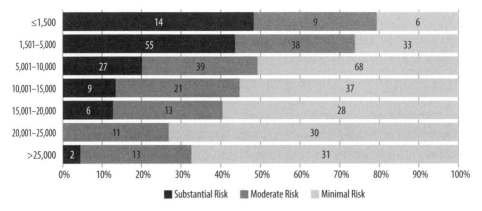

Figure 4.3. Number and percentage of Four-Year Public institutions in three risk categories based on Market Stress Test Scores by enrollment size bands.

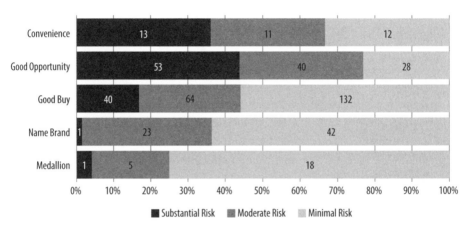

Figure 4.4. Number and percentage of Four-Year Public institutions in three risk categories based on Market Stress Test Scores by market segment.

Market Stress Test Scores among these public colleges and universities varied by size of institution as well (figure 4.3). Here the results were even more predictable. Only two public universities with enrollments exceeding 25,000 undergraduates experienced substantial risk, and three-quarters faced minimal or no risk. Smaller public institutions, however, face much bleaker futures. More than 40 percent of the public institutions in this category were rated as facing moderate to substantial risk.

The most differentiating category for this sector, however, was market segment which tracked six-year graduating rates (figure 4.4). Those institutions, Medallions and Name Brands, that are most successful in producing graduates and on average have the highest market prices, are the least likely to have scores indicating substantial risk. On the other hand, more than a third of the market's Convenience and Good Opportunity institutions—public colleges and universities with a less than 40 percent six-year graduation rate—are already experiencing substantial market risk.

The Four-Year Private Not-for-Profit Market

The Four-Year Private Not-for-Profit sector looks remarkably similar, though, as already noted, more institutions (62.1%) have Market Stress Test Scores that indicate just minimal risk (figure 4.5). But by 2016, a larger proportion of these private colleges and universities had lost more than 25 percent of the 2008 enrollments: 15 percent in this sector versus 9 percent in the Four-Year Public sector.

The regional distribution of risk resembled the distribution of risk that was characteristic of the Four-Year Public sector. Overall, however, market risk was more evenly distributed among the remaining regions.

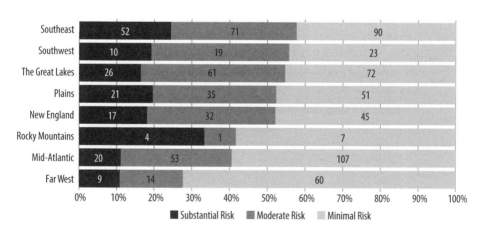

Figure 4.5. Number and percentage of Four-Year Private Not-for-Profit institutions in three risk categories based on Market Stress Test Scores by region.

Probably the greatest surprise is the relative health of New England institutions, which are often thought of as those facing the greatest risk of closure or forced consolidation. As in the Four-Year Public sector, the Far West (California, Washington, Oregon, Hawaii, and Nevada) proved the most stable region.

The starkest pattern of risk across the Four-Year Private Not-for-Profit sector reflects the importance of institutional size (figure 4.6). Institutions with fewer than 500 undergraduate enrollments were en route to becoming an endangered species. By 2016, 40 percent of these institutions were facing substantial risk, and only 20 percent were in

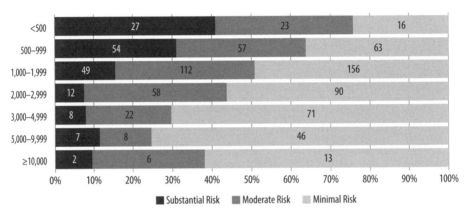

Figure 4.6. Number and percentage of Four-Year Private Not-for-Profit institutions in three risk categories based on Market Stress Test Scores by enrollment size bands.

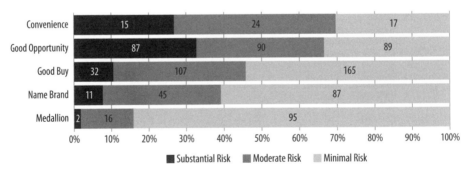

Figure 4.7. Number and percentage of Four-Year Private Not-for-Profit institutions in three risk categories based on Market Stress Test Scores by market segment.

the minimal risk category. Across the Four-Year Private Not-for-Profit sector bigger meant safer. Seventy-two percent of those with 5,000 or more undergraduates were scored as experiencing only minimal risk.

Market segment, as expected, proved an equally powerful predictor of market risk (figure 4.7). Medallion institutions were, for the most part, risk free—just two were scored as facing substantial risk. More than a quarter of the institutions in the Convenience and Good Opportunity segments faced substantial risk.

The Two-Year Public Market

The patterns we have been tracking diverge when the focus is on the market for Two-Year Public institutions. In the community college sector of the market, enrollment shifts are more common, most often tracking changes in the labor market. Between 2008 and 2016, a period that included both the recession of 2007–2008 and the 2013–2015 recovery, 16 percent of institutions in this sector experienced declines in the enrollments of degree- and certificate-seeking undergraduates of 25 percent or more. Forty-one percent reported enrollment declines of 10 percent or more.

Geographically, the distribution of risk in the Two-Year Public sector differs substantially from the distribution of risk in the Four-Year

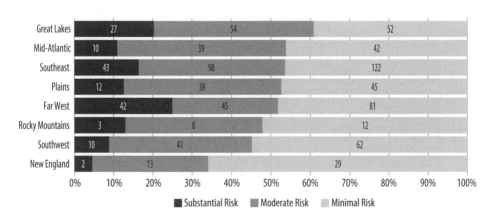

Figure 4.8. Number and percentage of Two-Year Public institutions in three risk categories based on Market Stress Test Scores by region.

Public and Four-Year Private Not-for-Profit sectors (figure 4.8). While risk in general is more prevalent among the two-year institutions, there is a smaller share of institutions at substantial risk than is found in the four-year sectors. It is across the Great Lakes, Mid-Atlantic, and Southeast regions that risk is most prevalent and least prevalent in New England, the Southwest, and Rocky Mountains. In contrast to the four-year sectors, the largest proportion of two-year institutions at substantial risk was in the Far West.

As elsewhere, substantial risk varied with size of institution, though the ordering is not as sharp (figure 4.9). Only among very big institutions—25,000 or more degree- and certificate-seeking students—

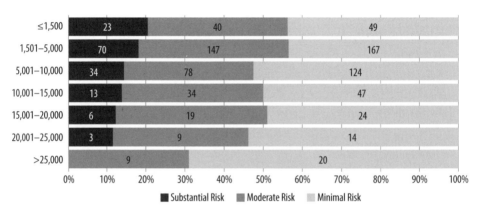

Figure 4.9. Number and percentage of Two-Year Public institutions in three risk categories based on Market Stress Test Scores by enrollment size bands.

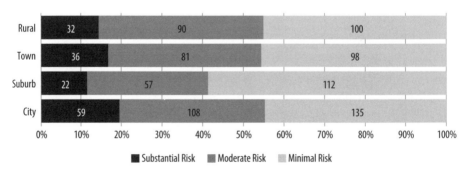

Figure 4.10. Number and percentage of Two-Year Public institutions in three risk categories based on Market Stress Test Scores by degree of urbanization.

was there likely to be substantial enrollment stability. We also tested whether degree of urbanization might have made a difference, but it didn't, except that suburban institutions were less likely to experience substantial risk than other community colleges (figure 4.10).

An Important Set of Answers

The analysis of the distribution of market risk across higher education's three main markets—Four-Year Public, Four-Year Private Not-for-Profit, and Two-Year Public—confirms the basic findings about the trajectory of these markets we presented in chapter 3. It is a winners' market. The institutions least likely to experience market stress are those at the top of the pecking order. Those are the institutions that have the status and prestige, along with the financial resources, to buck the headwinds generated by a public unhappy with the direction and quality of the enterprise. The winners are bigger and more prestigious than other institutions in their segment, more likely to be either East Coast or West Coast, and more financially secure. Among public institutions, both Four- and Two-Year, substantial risk was most often a function of decreasing public appropriations.

There were few surprises except to note that the two-year community college market proved to be the least differentiated by the key variables that our Market Stress Test Scores employed. Few institutions and even fewer policy wonks should be surprised by our findings. Across the markets that served students interested in a four-year undergraduate education there continues to be modest growth in the number of students. To be sure, there are institutions whose futures are in doubt, but they are a distinct minority. By our reckoning, the bottom of the market is limited to 20 percent or less of competing institutions.

The big, most important news concerns what is not happening. There is simply no evidence that the market is being disrupted. There are no Sears or JCPenney, no iconic brands that have lost their way. At the same time, there are no emerging icons to challenge the markets' historic leaders. Neither Southern New Hampshire University nor Arizona State University have claim to that distinction though they will no doubt argue to the contrary. As we observed in chapter 2, the 2,300-plus institutions that compete for undergraduate enrollments do so in a consolidating market. The old rules of thumb for separating winners and losers are as reliable today as they were 50 years ago when the enterprise first discovered the allure of rankings.

Having come to that conclusion, we also were interested in how the market was treating the key student populations that have become the focus of much of the policy discussion that now swirls around American higher education: students of color, students with limited economic resources (and, hence, Pell eligible), and students 25 years and older. Here there are also few surprises. We start with the totals of African American, Hispanic, and Asian students reported by individual institutions in their 2016 IPEDS filings (figure 4.11). We asked a simple question of each group. What percentage of undergraduate students in each demographic group was reported to be attending institutions that our analysis judged to be at substantial market risk? We also disaggregated those results by market sector: Four-Year Public, Four-Year Private Not-for-Profit, and Two-Year Public.

In each of the three sectors, African American students were the group most likely to attend an institution at substantial risk. Among undergraduates attending a Four-Year Public university or college,

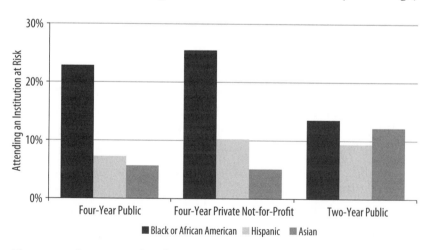

Figure 4.11. Percentage of students attending an institution at substantial risk based on Market Stress Test Scores by ethnicity and sector.

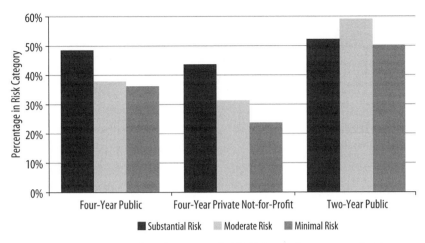

Figure 4.12. Percentage of students awarded Pell Grants by sector and risk category based on Market Stress Test Scores.

African American students were two and a half times more likely to attend an institution at substantial risk than Hispanic students. Compared to Asian students, African Americans were more than three times more likely to enroll in an institution facing substantial enrollment risk.

The percentage of full-time first-time students attending a four-year institution who were awarded a Pell Grant highlights the degree to which institutions most at risk are also those institutions with the largest percentage of their students with a Pell Grant (figure 4.12). Two-Year Public colleges and universities were the most dependent on the Pell program, but an institution's Market Stress Test Score did not predict Pell eligibility as was the case among baccalaureate institutions.

The distribution of students 25 years and older tells a slightly different story (figure 4.13). Adult students are slightly more likely to attend a baccalaureate institution facing substantial risk than not—particularly among Four-Year Private Not-for-Profit institutions. In the community college sector, there are more adult students, and they are more evenly distributed across the risk categories.

It is the distribution of these three categories of students (racial/ethnic minority, Pell eligible, older) among colleges and universities at

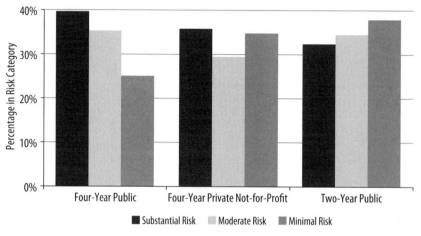

Figure 4.13. Percentage of undergraduates 25 and older by sector and risk category based on Market Stress Test Scores.

risk that creates what can best be described as a policy conundrum, one that lacks a straightforward resolution. Even though the market now clearly advantages institutions that are big and rich, the policy temptation will be to let market forces trim higher education's roster of undergraduate institutions. While the number of closures and forced mergers and consolidations will likely increase over the next decade, the actual numbers will be relatively modest while the overall shape of the enterprise will be little changed. Leaving the market on autopilot becomes a viable option, in part, because of the failure of public initiatives to reshape the market for an undergraduate education. Witness the mess that resulted from the policy wonks' attack on the for-profit industry. No one would suggest that the consequence of those initiatives was anything but disjointed and, ultimately, dismally counterproductive.

However, the maldistribution of market risk matters, as it turns out, a lot. If the market is allowed to prune higher education of its less successful enterprises, the result might well be a system that is more hostile to African Americans, less attractive to students who qualify for Pell awards, and, to a lesser extent, less welcoming to adult learners. That is the implication of the overrepresentation of African American and economically disadvantaged students (as measured by Pell eligibility) at institutions facing substantial market risks now and into the immediate future.

Some, we suspect, will argue that the solution lies in providing sufficient federal subsidies to shore up those institutions most threatened. It would make sense, for example, to use the 60-plus billion dollars required to eliminate most, if not all, community college tuition charges to instead provide direct grants to those same institutions to improve their capacity to graduate students and to graduate them on time. The politics of direct federal grants to institutions are such that the processes and procedures necessary to launch such a program, and then ensure its continuing quality, for the moment at least, are beyond the nation's capacity to enact such a program.

Thus, we are back where we started. It is clear that the market as currently organized works against the disadvantaged students in general and African Americans and those with Pell eligibility in particular. In the kind of consolidating market that now shapes the enterprise, we know what is likely to happen whether we like it or not. A modest first step to counter those trends would be to focus on gaining a better understanding of how the undergraduate enrollment market functions along with a more nuanced understanding of just which institutions now need to ask themselves, "Is it closing time?"

FIVE

Winners and Losers

ULTIMATELY, IT IS institutional futures that matter—who survives, who prospers, and as we just noted, who must ask, "Is it closing time?" We have calculated Market Stress Test Scores for just over 2,300 colleges and universities—Four-Year Private Not-for Profit, Four-Year Public, and Two-Year Public. Collectively, they yield the market portraits presented in chapter 4. At the same time, these Market Stress Test Scores tell a wide variety of individual stories that nonetheless conform to the organizing principles that govern today's market for an undergraduate education—largely that success means getting bigger and richer and, as far as possible, drawing students from growing markets in the East and Far West of the United States.

What It Means to Be a Winner in a Consolidating Market

The easiest tales to tell are those of the institutions at the top of the baccalaureate college market. They are the Medallions, colleges and universities with high graduation rates, substantial endowments, and excess applicant pools. Figure 5.1 presents the Market Stress Test Score for a private East Coast Medallion university. Figure 5.1A and 5.1C portray a university that has continuously enrolled ever more students, 95 percent of whom will continue to be enrolled as sophomores. The

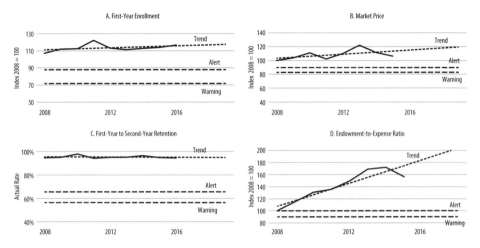

Figure 5.1. Components of the Market Stress Test Score for a private East Coast Medallion university.

university's pricing strategy, of steady increases in excess of inflation expressed in constant 2008 dollars (figure 5.1B), yields substantial increases in revenue per student and hence substantial net tuition income. During the 2008–2016 period, the value of the university's endowment (in actual rather than in constant dollars) increased substantially— nearly 70 percent—while expenses were held to a 7 percent increase. What is most noticeable about figure 5.1 is that all the trend lines are positive, and the trend line for market price is markedly so.

The trend lines for a neighboring Medallion liberal arts college are similarly positive, though less so. Unlike the Medallion university discussed first, this college displays a trend line for market price that is steady (in constant dollars) rather than increasing. For the institution portrayed in figure 5.2, the key variable to follow is indeed price, in part reflecting market pressures and in part a decision to increase its financial aid budget in order to enroll economically disadvantaged students.

Public Medallions mirror the experiences of the private Medallions— nearly everyone is a winner. Still, there are important differences. The Market Stress Test Score for a southeastern public Medallion university is presented in figure 5.3. Look at figure 5.3D. The problem facing this Medallion research university is the diminishing support

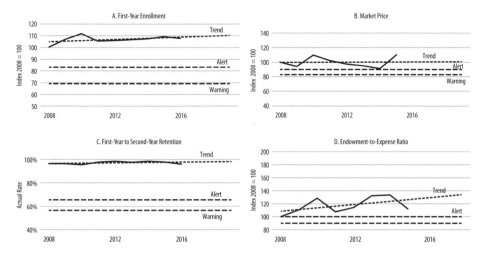

Figure 5.2. Components of the Market Stress Test Score for a private East Coast Medallion liberal arts college.

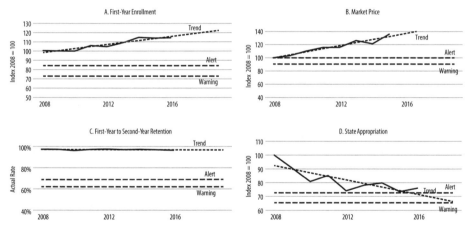

Figure 5.3. Components of the Market Stress Test Score for a southeastern public Medallion university.

supplied by its state. Those missing funds are balanced, for the moment, by enrollment growth (figure 5.3A) and market price increases (figure 5.3B). If state support continues to decline, or if the institution cannot continue to grow its undergraduate student body or charge ever-increasing market prices, the institution will likely face future challenges.

Big winners among the nation's Two-Year Public institutions are harder to find given the boom-and-bust cycle of enrollments occasioned by the 2007–2013 recession and recovery. Tight employment markets inevitably track with community college enrollment contractions no matter how successful or innovative an institution is. Figure 5.4 plots the experience of a large (nearly 20,000 students) Southeastern community college from a state known for its innovative community college system. Two of the three graphs reflect the sine-wave-like patterns characteristic of almost all Two-Year Public institutions for which we have sufficient data to develop a Market Stress Test Score. In the case of the institution portrayed in figure 5.4, enrollments have remained strong and, most important, public funding has actually increased since 2008. Problematic fluctuations in net tuition revenue to instructional costs periodically take this ratio below the alert line as the institution has struggled to control instructional expenditures. It is also important to remember there are only three variables in the Two-Year Public Market Stress Tests: new students, net tuition revenue to instructional cost, and state and local funding. As a result, the maximum negative Market Stress Test Score an individual institution can receive is 9, rather than the maximum of 12 for four-year institutions.

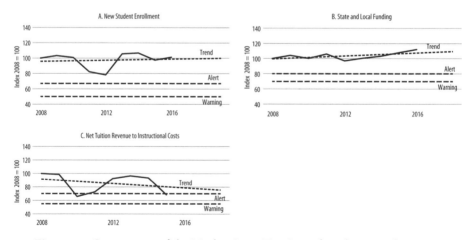

Figure 5.4. Components of the Market Stress Test Score for a large southeastern community college.

The Substantial Risks Losers Face

The losers in these markets are equally easy to spot—there are no real surprises, only the fact that there are so few institutions with Market Stress Test Scores of 6 or above, and still fewer four-year institutions scoring 9 or above. Figure 5.5 presents the Market Stress Test Score for a southwestern community college with fewer than 1,000 students. The dominant feature of figure 5.5 is the relentless downward slopes of the three graphs—everything is heading in the wrong direction.

Figure 5.6 presents a southeastern community college of some 1,300 total students in slightly less trouble though it, too, is classified as being at substantial risk. The principal difference reflected in the two figures is the ability of the southeastern community college to keep its expenses roughly in line with its tuition revenue (see figure 5.6C). Nevertheless, while the tuition to instructional cost ratio and the projected trend into the future are well above the alert line, the future of the institution remains a concern in light of the trajectory of the other two risk components.

The segment of the market in the most peril is that served by Four-Year Private Not-for-Profit colleges and universities. The first example of an institution at risk is the small (less than 300 students) Far

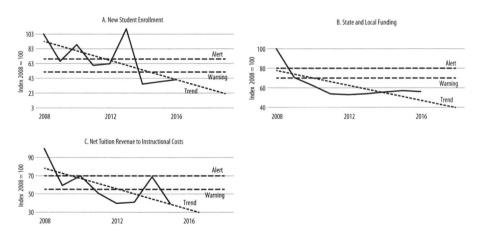

Figure 5.5. Components of the Market Stress Test Score for a southwestern community college with fewer than 1,000 students.

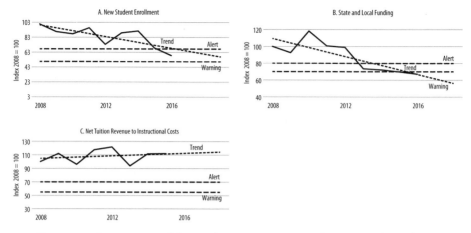

Figure 5.6. Components of the Market Stress Test Score for an at-risk southeastern community college.

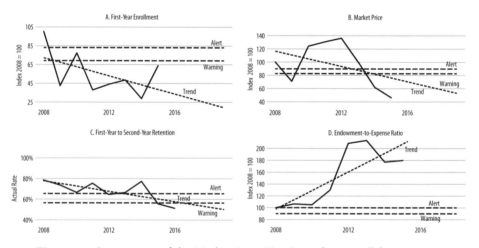

Figure 5.7. Components of the Market Stress Test Score for a small far western liberal arts college.

West liberal arts college portrayed in figure 5.7. Its Market Stress Test Score was a 9, suggesting that a lot has already gone wrong. In three of the four graphs of figure 5.7, the data end up below the warning line, indicating the institution is operating in troubled waters. This school is already failing to attract sufficient numbers of first-year students and may be close to not having sufficient mass to operate as a fully accredited institution. The college loses more than 40 percent of its freshmen during their first year at the institution. It has tried deep discounting as a way to maintain its enrollment, but even a sharply declining market price has not reversed its enrollment losses.

Figure 5.7D appears to be good news but is misleading. While its endowment-to-expense ratio shows a decidedly upward slope, its endowment is small, and it has been forced to implement significant cost reductions in view of decreased income due to enrollment losses and the deep tuition discounting.

It is not only the nation's tiny colleges that are at substantial risk. Figure 5.8 presents the Market Stress Test Score for a small New England liberal arts college with just over a thousand undergraduates now in financial difficulty. Here first-year first-time enrollment is in the danger zone between the alert and warning lines. Although the college has significantly reduced its market price, its freshman enrollment continues to decline. On the positive side, it has actually increased its freshman-to-sophomore retention rate. As in the case of the small Far West liberal arts college in figure 5.7, the improving endowment-to-costs ratio is something of a statistical artifact. The worrisome state of affairs for this institution is depicted most clearly by its decreasing enrollments and market price.

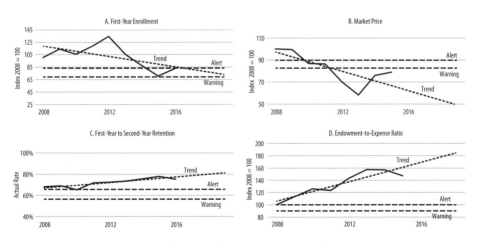

Figure 5.8. Components of the Market Stress Test Score for a New England liberal arts college.

Figure 5.9 presents the Market Stress Test Score for a specialized Four-Year Private Not-for-Profit univesity located in a major urban center. Its problems are not materially different from the institutions portrayed in figures 5.7 and 5.8, though it enjoys a student body of more that 5,000 undergraduates. It is losing new first-year enrollments, and while the retention trajectory appears positive, the decline in the retention rate of the last few years could augur future problems for retaining those first-year students who do enroll. For financial reasons, it has stuck with an aggressive pricing strategy that has seen its market price increase by 20 percent over the last five years. The changes in its endowment-to-expense ratio is largely a function of a major scandal involving fraudulent investments made on behalf of its endowment. In sum, no good news here.

Overall, there is a larger percentage, but a smaller number of Four-Year Public colleges and universities than either Two-Year Public or Four-Year Private Not-for-Profit receiving Market Stress Test Scores of 4 or more, marking them as institutions at substantial risk. (The number of institutions in the Four-Year Public sector is considerably smaller than the number in either of the other two sectors.) Nonetheless, those Four-Year Public institutions receiving scores of 4 or more face the same challenges as their Four-Year Private Not-for-Profit

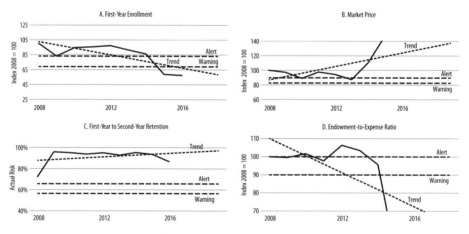

Figure 5.9. Components of the Market Stress Test Score for a larger specialized private not-for-profit urban university.

counterparts. The Market Stress Test Score profiles for three institutions follow: a midsized midwestern comprehensive university that was held hostage to its state's budgetary shortfall, a second midwestern university in an area of the country with bleak enrollment prospects, and a larger southwestern state university that has somewhat unexpectedly found itself facing a substantial enrollment shortfall. We begin with the institution whose budget, along with those of the state's other public comprehensive institutions, has become a bargaining chip in a multiyear legislative battle.

Nothing seems to be going right for this institution of just under 7,000 students. As depicted in figure 5.10, its first-year class was 40 percent smaller in 2016 than it was in 2008. Retention, while projected to stay above the alert line, declined as well. An aggressive investment in more discounting yielded a 15 percent reduction in the university's market price and a corresponding reduction in operating funds. The institution's biggest problem was the near absence of state funding. The result was a Market Stress Test Score of 9, the second highest our methodology awarded. (No institution scored a 10 or 11.) It was scant consolation that the highest score of 12 was awarded to another public institution in the same state.

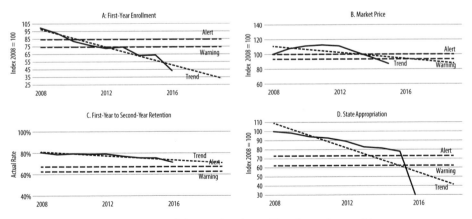

Figure 5.10. Components of the Market Stress Test Score for a midwestern comprehensive public university.

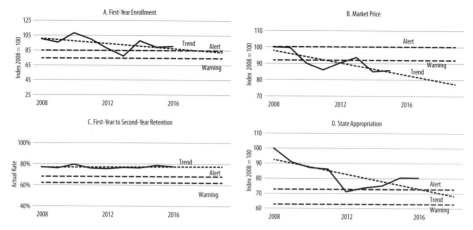

Figure 5.11. Components of the Market Stress Test Score for a traditional midwestern public comprehensive university.

Two public comprehensive universities, the midwestern campus portrayed in figure 5.11 and a southwestern one in figure 5.12, have fared somewhat better, but nonetheless face worrisome prospects. The midwestern institution has the advantage of being relatively large. In 2016, it reported having just under 20,000 undergraduates. Its loss of new students is not quite as severe as those of the school in figure 5.10, and retention of freshmen has not yet proved to be a problem. Nonetheless, there has been the same reliance on aggressive discounting with much the same result—a 15 percent reduction in the tuition revenue that has failed to stem the loss in first-year enrollments.

The southwestern university in figure 5.12 is suffering more serious erosion of its freshman class and similarly is relying on an unsuccessful discounting strategy. In the case of each of these two institutions, there has been a loss of state funding that has recently been reversed by additional appropriations. Those increases, however, have not been sufficient to restore state funding to their 2008 levels.

No Surprises Here

Like the distribution of risk described in chapter 4, the experiences of individual institutions, both winners and losers, are pretty much what

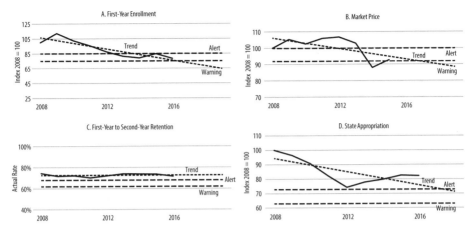

Figure 5.12. Components of the Market Stress Test Score for a southwestern public university.

one would expect given the history of American higher education over the last half century. The winners are the Medallions, institutions that will continue to strengthen as the market further consolidates. Their worries are principally political—have their ever-higher market prices made them targets, not just of envy, but of political action as well? There are more Private Not-for-Profit winners than Public winners, but in the end, the latter serve more students at often substantially lower market prices.

The losers—those institutions already at substantial risk—owe their bad luck to a grab bag of unexpected consequences. For most Four-Year Public institutions, it is their states that have erected the most troubling barriers, almost exclusively in the form of dramatically declining state appropriations—and in a few cases, an elimination of appropriations due to legislative and political deadlocks. But there are other causes as well, including the mismanagement of endowment funds, and adopting risky pricing strategies that yield both ever higher discount rates and little or no increase in enrolling students. The really unlucky institutions have suffered a double whammy over the last decade—higher discount rates that yield less tuition income per student coupled with enrollment declines yielding ever fewer new students and substantially less net tuition income. Most losers have also experienced financial shifts large enough that budget reductions alone are unlikely to yield sufficient savings to offset losses in revenue.

Again, what surprises us most is just how predictable these results are. The basic structure of the market—in which the students with the highest prematriculation probability of earning a baccalaureate degree are most likely to attend the biggest and wealthiest institutions—remains largely unchanged. By and large students of color, and African American students in particular, are overrepresented among the institutions we have judged to be at substantial risk. And, if the past is a predictor of future trends, community colleges will continue to experience boom-and-bust cycles closely tied to economic fluctuations and shifts in the labor market. Private For-Profit institutions will likely experience further turbulence, in part as a function of their own missteps, in part due to an uncertain political climate that alternately punishes and rewards them, and in part because of the floundering that is now a by-product of their search for alternate business models and their deployment of new, tech-dependent teaching modalities.

The mysteries that are of interest here are neither at the top nor at the bottom of the market but, rather, in the middle. We turn next to market stress facing the institutions we have dubbed *those that are bound to struggle.*

SIX

Those Who Are Bound to Struggle

IN COMPETITIVE MARKETS, the focus is often on the winners and losers. The former become the hallmarks of the future; the latter serve as models for lessons learned. In today's retail market, the winners are Amazon and Walmart, the losers are Sears and JCPenney. More often the competitive reality is more complex—and that is certainly the case for the competition for first-year undergraduates. From this perspective, the really interesting stories focus not on the top or bottom of the market but, rather, on its middle, filled with institutions that in the past have proved their resilience but now are struggling to secure their futures.

Although each has its own story to tell, what our Market Stress Test Scores capture, both arithmetically and graphically, is a reality in which there are a limited number of market indicators that gauge just how much of a struggle a given institution is likely to face. This chapter presents the market graphics for a sample of institutions from each of the three sectors that encompass nearly all of the market for an undergraduate education in the United States: Four-Year Private Not-for-Profit, Four-Year Public, and Two-Year Public. Taken both together and separately, the experiences of these institutions highlight the questions that struggling colleges and universities need to ask themselves as they develop strategies to change their futures.

Market Price and New Student Enrollments in the Mixed World of Private Institutions

First up. That class of institutions most often described as being challenged—the 200-plus private colleges and universities, whose Market Stress Test Scores indicate they now face moderate risk and might well face more substantial risk in the future. We start with a truly small college of less than 500 students, where there have been dramatic swings in the number of new students enrolled (figure 6.1A) along with somewhat improving freshman-to-sophomore student retention (figure 6.1C), noting that for the most recent year, its retention rate was just barely in the danger zone between the alert and warning lines.

The most pressing challenge this college faces is reflected in the downward slope of its market price. The message of figure 6.1B is that the market has continued to discount the institution's worth, requiring the institution to set a market price that, by 2016, had fallen below the warning line and was on track to decline further. The short-term lesson is that past reductions in market price had not stemmed the loss of first-year students. Its Market Stress Test Score of 6 (out of 12) ought to tell

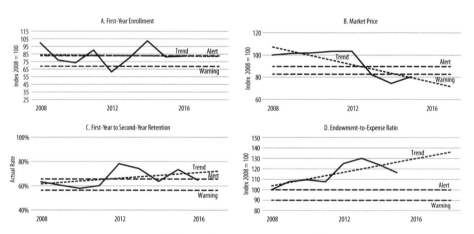

Figure 6.1. Components of the Market Stress Test Score for a small private liberal arts college.

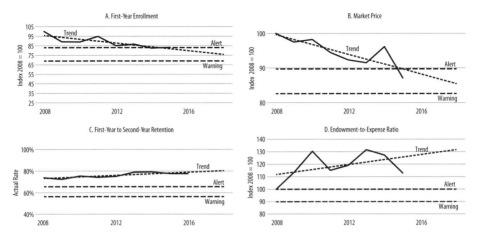

Figure 6.2. Components of the Market Stress Test Score for a larger career-oriented private university.

the campus community that the college has already drifted into a state of substantial risk.

A different though related pattern is reflected in figure 6.2, which graphs the Market Stress Test Score for a medium-sized (more than 6,000 undergraduates) northeastern private university that focuses on career and technical education. Like the school depicted in figure 6.1, the institution whose Market Stress Test Score is reflected in figure 6.2 faces a double whammy: the number of first-year students has continued to decline despite the institution's cutting its market price. Again, the first lesson to be learned is that neither increased discounting nor additional merit financial aid will likely stabilize enrollment. Where the institution portrayed in figure 6.2 is most different from the institution portrayed in figure 6.1 is in its healthy first-year to second-year retention rate and its relatively positive but somewhat volatile financial profile.

A third example of this interplay between the size of the first-year freshman class and the inability of price reductions to stem the loss of new students is portrayed in figure 6.3. This institution is a midsize Catholic college with just under 3,000 undergraduates. As in our first

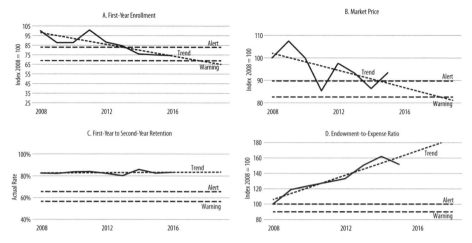

Figure 6.3. Components of the Market Stress Test Score for a small to midsize Catholic college.

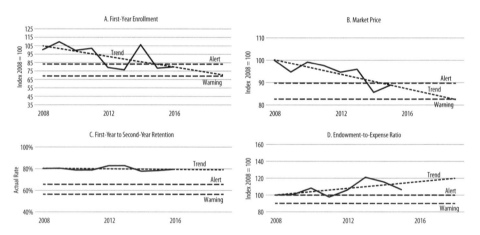

Figure 6.4. Components of the Market Stress Test Score for a midwestern liberal arts college.

two examples, enrolling first-year (freshman) undergraduates at a sustainable market price has become a major challenge as shown by the institution's downward drift on both measures. Retention, however, is not a problem and the institution's finances are stable, with a positive endowment-to-expense ratio trend. This same pattern is replicated in figure 6.4, which portrays the experience of a midwestern liberal arts college of 1,200 students.

The Quest for Stable Government Funding Facing Public Colleges and Universities

Public institutions that struggle face many of the same issues but with a twist: what triggers risk most often is a persistent decline in public funding. Figure 6.5 presents the Market Stress Test Score for a large (nearly 30,000 undergraduates) urban university in the Northeast. For this institution, there is substantial good news. Enrollment of new, first-year students has grown steadily which, combined with an increasing freshman-to-sophomore retention rate has yielded a steady growth in the overall size of the undergraduate student body. The price the institution has paid for this good news, however, is a dangerous reduction in market price. This pattern of declining public support and market price reductions will not likely prove financially sustainable over the long run.

In contrast, the suburban university depicted in figure 6.6 has half the enrollment of the institution in figure 6.5 and is in the Midwest rather than in the Northeast; nonetheless, this school has a nearly identical Market Stress Test Score reflecting increasing enrollment and stable retention but a persistently declining market price matched by a declining state appropriation.

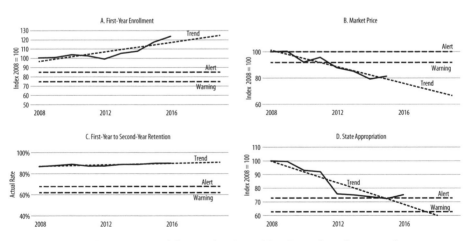

Figure 6.5. Components of the Market Stress Test Score for a large northeastern urban university.

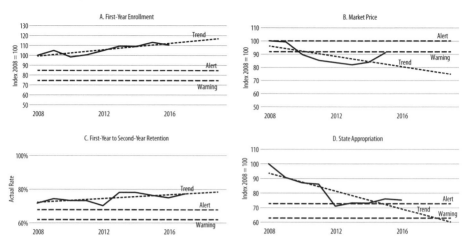

Figure 6.6. Components of the Market Stress Test Score for a midwestern suburban university.

The experience of colleges and universities within systems can also differ from one to another. Among the 23 California State Universities belonging to the CSU system, for example, only three had Market Stress Test Scores, indicating that the institutions faced moderate risk and none crossed the substantial risk threshold. No institution within the University of California system had a Market Stress Test Score greater than 2, and the component in those cases that triggered a moderate risk score was a declining state appropriation. The SUNY colleges and universities resemble their CSU counterparts: only 3 face substantial risk and none have a Market Stress Test Score greater than 5. In sharp contrast, among the 14 institutions composing Pennsylvania's State System of Higher Education (PASSHE), just 4 were scored as facing minimal risk, another 2 as facing moderate risk (figure 6.7), and 7 as facing substantial risk. The 14th PASSHE institution had a Market Stress Test Score of 9, indicating truly substantial risk and likely to face closure, at least later, if not sooner. The differences among the outcomes for schools in these systems is likely the result of the geographic differences in the pool of college applicants discussed in earlier chapters and differences in state and local politics that influence these local systems in unique ways.

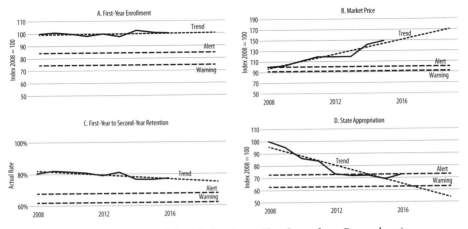

Figure 6.7. Components of the Market Stress Test Score for a Pennsylvania State System of Higher Education university facing moderate risk.

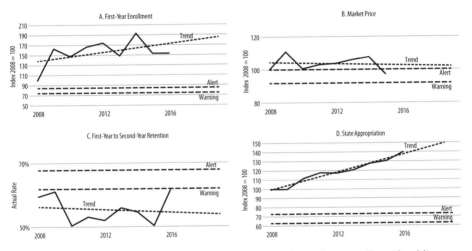

Figure 6.8. Components of the Market Stress Test Score for a small rural public university.

There were, scattered among the country's Four-Year Public institutions, a host of interesting exceptions to the general pattern of market stress being principally related to a decline of state appropriation. Among small, rural institutions, the problem was often retention, as in the case of the institution depicted in figure 6.8. Still, the dominant patterns involve public institutions compensating for declining public appropriations by attempting to increase both market price and first-year (freshman) enrollments. When that strategy fails, as in the case of 8 of the PASSHE institutions, substantial market stress is the result.

Amid the Traditional Ebb and Flow of Community College Enrollments

The market stress patterns for the nation's Two-Year Public institutions, in part, tracks with the dominant pattern among Four-Year Public institutions: real declines in the market price the institution can charge along with continued declines in public funding, sometimes ameliorated by increased first-year enrollments. But the pattern is also more complicated because of the traditional ebb and flow of community college enrollments: up during a recession, back down once the economy picks up steam. Given the economic realities between 2008 and 2016 (the years for which we have data), one result is that nearly 150 of the community colleges in our data set cross the threshold to substantial risk. On the other hand, community colleges have more experience with the ups and downs of enrollments and seem less bothered by them.

Figures 6.9 and 6.10 depict two community colleges that have Market Stress Test Scores of 4. The first one is a large, midwestern college with strong ties to local manufacturing. During the recession, it bulked up its enrollments, although those seem to be returning to their 2008 level. Its tuitions and fees are politically constrained, yielding an imbalance between revenue and expense—a situation exacerbated by declining funding from the state. The struggle for this institution involves returning its public funding to prerecession levels.

Figure 6.10 displays the Market Stress Test Score for an even larger (nearly 20,000 students) community college in California. Enrollments, having dropped below the warning line following the recession, started to recover while its state and local funding stabilized. What this institution requires, as do most public institutions in our data set, is a return to public funding at a prerecession level.

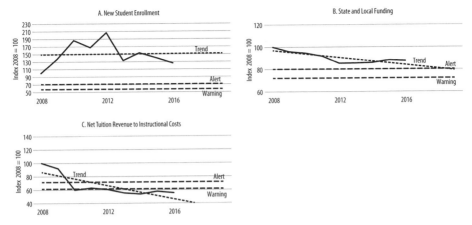

Figure 6.9. Components of the Market Stress Test Score for a large community college in the industrial heartland.

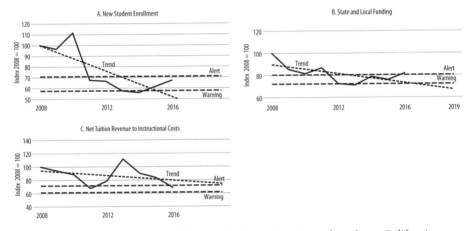

Figure 6.10. Components of the Market Stress Test Score for a large California community college.

Making Sense of It All

Most surprising about the futures of struggling colleges and universities, both public and private, both four year and two year, is the consistency of the challenges they face. Four-year institutions, at or near the bottom of the market, face the prospect of not being able to raise their market prices sufficiently to offset enrollment shortfalls, which could become ever more severe as more and more students choose to "shop up" in a consolidating market. For public institutions, second is the specter of continuing declines in public funding. And even struggling private, not-for-profit institutions will be impacted to the extent they are dependent on state-funded student aid programs that may now be equally at risk.

For the baccalaureate market, the remaining challenge involves retention. At the top of the market, freshmen are routinely expected to transition to sophomore status and, ultimately, to graduate. Nonetheless, the data suggest that on many campuses, there is a real gap between that expectation and the reality for many students. Most institutions could more than make up for their enrollment shortfalls, by increasing their ability to retain the students they recruit and enroll. The problem is that most of these institutions simply don't know how.

SEVEN

Changing the Slope

W E UNDERSTAND WELL that identifying the components of market risk, while an important contribution to the conversation, will not be sufficient for many reading this book. The most likely reaction, particularly from institutional leaders who know their school's sustainability is at risk, will be, "Tell me something I don't know. What I need are strategies that offer the promise of fixing my problems." This is a tall order, of course. Given that the problem is market (and not necessarily institutionally) driven, there are no magic bullets in this game. Nonetheless, the fixed nature of the market, as best reflected in the correlation of the Market Stress Test Scores with geography, size, and market segment, provides important clues as to what a rejuvenating strategy might look like.

We begin with a reminder of the two caveats with which we began our analysis. First, our task has not been to predict which institutions are likely to close or merge but, rather, to identify which institutions are most likely to face substantial market risk. Our hope is that some of the institutions we have identified as facing serious problems—roughly speaking those colleges and universities with Market Stress Test Scores in the 4–5 range—will right themselves following some of the advice we are about to offer.

Our second caveat concerns our definition of the market as the sum total of those currently enrolled in a college or a university. As we noted earlier, it is a definition that focuses on buyers rather than shoppers. It is also a definition that doesn't account for the possibility that substantial numbers of would-be undergraduates are not currently enrolled in a college or university. Some have argued that non-college-degree completers represent a pool of potential shoppers who can be converted into actual buyers. Those who are familiar with the history of Southwest Airlines will recall that reaching out to unserved populations living in often ignored locations accounted for much of that airline's early successes. It was a classic "Blue Ocean" strategy, which allowed Southwest to avoid head-to-head competition with the nation's legacy airlines. There are higher education commentators and pundits who would have institutions with enrollment shortfalls reach out almost exclusively to older learners and those who started but never completed a college degree. It is a strategy, however, that assumes institutions at risk are more flexible and willing to innovate than they have proved to be in the past.

Our findings, however, make clear that the market is neither a mystery nor likely to be either recast or disrupted. The basic seams that organize the market are both fixed and well known. Prestige matters. Rankings matter. Geography and history play important roles in defining an individual institution's place in the market. If anything, that market is becoming more rather than less fixed, making it increasingly likely that it will be the richer and bigger institutions that reap the benefits of a consolidating market. There is nothing in the market data we have explored to suggest a different future, only that institutions at the top of the market will likely substitute future growth in volume for past growth in price. For public institutions, there is the further risk of continued shortfalls in state and local funding, whether the result of downturns in their state's economy or the triumph of political factions opposed to the tax increases necessary to restore state and local funding to prerecession levels.

Thus, we circle back to the question with which we began, which institutions ought to be asking, Is it closing time? Those institutions most at risk did not need our analysis to tell them they are in trouble. They have known for some time that, absent a miracle, the end is near. For these institutions, our work will prove more confirming than revealing.

The winners, we suspect, already know that their futures are secure, though there are those within their communities who have been made anxious by the gloom and doom of the prognosticators. What such institutions can learn here is the import of pricing policy, the necessity for continued fund-raising, and, if the institution is dependent on public funding, the wisdom of effective lobbying.

We do believe, however, that our analysis can provide important guidance to those institutions whose Market Stress Test Scores identify them as a struggling institution. For these colleges and universities, a Market Stress Test Score can be both diagnostic and prescriptive, telling them what needs to change and why. The model underlying the Market Stress Test Scores is both simple and broadly applicable, differing for the most part only in detail across a full range of institutions. The prescriptive advice that we have derived from the model we hope will prove similarly applicable.

What to Look for in a Market Stress Test Score Graphic

All the diagnostic information a Market Stress Test Score provides is contained within its accompanying graphic. Scores at or above 4 indicate an institution that is likely to face substantial risk; scores at 6 or above are most worrisome since the higher the score, the greater the probability of real trouble ahead. More important, the Market Stress Test Score components indicate the principal levers an institution might have for altering its future.

For Four-Year Private Not-for-Profit Institutions:
First-Year First-Time
First-Year to Second-Year Retention
Market Price
Endowment-to-Expense Ratio

For Four-Year Public Institutions:
  First-Year First-Time
  First-Year to Second-Year Retention
  Market Price
  State Appropriation
Two-Year Public Institutions:
  New Student Enrollment
  Net Tuition Revenue to Instructional Cost
  State and Local Funding

None of these levers should be surprising. Besides serving as the main components of our Market Stress Test Scores, they are found on most of the dashboards provosts and deans have on their desktop computers. What our analysis has added to this mix is the importance the Market Stress Test Score assigns to the slope of the trend line that measures change over time. What makes the slope important is that institutional cost structures are too often inflexible, making the implementation of a change strategy both time consuming and politically difficult. The challenge nearly every institution with a Market Stress Test Score of 4 or above now confronts is the need to implement actions that change each of its downward slopes.

As we have already noted, identifying the slopes that have to be changed is not enough. What any campus community taking our work seriously would want to know is how to change a trajectory that literally has been a decade or more in the making—and to make those changes despite the institutional inertia that often robs good ideas of their necessary urgency. We also need to acknowledge that neither the IPEDS data nor our presentation of them offer much help in identifying the strategies that will make institutional recovery possible. The strategies that follow instead derive from more than a decade of working directly with institutions, first under the banner of the Pew Higher Education Roundtable and subsequently as part of the Learning Alliance for Higher Education. Much of what we will suggest was first raised in a series of monographs, beginning with *The Structure of College Choice* (Zemsky and Oedel 1983) and *Higher Education as Com-*

petitive Enterprise (Zemsky, Shaman, and Shapiro 2001) and, more recently, in *Checklist for Change* (Zemsky 2013) and *The Market Imperative* (Zemsky and Shaman 2017).

Our proposed strategies fall into two broad categories: (1) those that focus on market strategies, including pricing policies, and (2) those that involve changes in internal institutional behavior that hold out the promise of substantially improving an institution's marketing and retention of first-year first-time student learners. We begin with the former because increasing new student enrollment is the more obvious short-term solution to the problems facing institutions at substantial risk.

It's All about the Price

We have assumed that nearly all institutions facing shortfalls of new students have tried improved marketing. They have hired consultants who promise analytic insights as to why so many student shoppers buy their higher educations elsewhere. They have invested in new marketing materials. They have hired new staff, having first made their chief enrollment officers vice presidents. And, their Market Stress Test Score reports attest they have engaged in ever more substantial price discounting in an attempt to lure more students to their campuses.

The institutions in the most trouble are those that have declining enrollments and declining market prices. Where both slopes are persistently negative, drifting below the alert line into what we have identified as the danger zone, we suspect that the institution slid into pricing practices designed to attract more students by further discounting the sticker price. And when those price reductions do not yield increased enrollments, the institution is saddled with unsustainable pricing practices, even in the short run.

A growing number of colleges have concluded that the spanner in the works is the now decades-old practice of having a high sticker price, which is ameliorated for almost all students—in many institutions truly all undergraduates—with generous amounts of student financial aid, which, in all but name, are price discounts. What is needed, they proclaim, is not a high-price/high-aid pricing model but instead a low-price/low-aid pricing model. Moving from the old model to the new is called a *tuition reset.*

While a host of private colleges, often spurred on by trustees tired of defending escalating sticker prices, have talked about resetting their tuitions, to date fewer than 30 have implemented the change. That most tuition resets have occurred in the last five years has made it difficult to judge whether such changes are yielding stabilized enrollments and net tuition revenue sufficient to cover operating costs. There have been less than a handful of credible studies, two of which were dissertations by administrators turned graduate students enrolled in University of Pennsylvania's Executive Doctorate in Higher Education Management Program. Both asked the same basic question: Is a tuition reset worth the disruption and risk that accompanies it?

The first study was by Laura Casamento, at the time Utica College's executive vice president and now the college's president. Researched and written while Utica College was in the process of considering a tuition reset, Casamento's study was a cautionary tale, warning institutions considering a tuition reset to be both cautious and purposeful.

> Most colleges and universities that have implemented a tuition price reset strategy have done so with negative or mixed results, because the strategy was not part of a larger, comprehensive strategy to elevate the brand of the institution. Comprehensive strategies require linkages to academic quality and program delivery, investment in institutional branding, revenue diversification and risk mitigation. Implementing a tuition price reset as a stand-alone strategy causes the decision to be viewed through a single lens, where price—and only price—is the story. (Casamento 2016, 74)

Casamento's advice is worth remembering. Each of the two institutions in her sample of five whose tuition resets produced the sought-after stabilization of net tuition revenue had "a story to tell in terms of investment and enrollment growth" in the form of larger freshman classes, new buildings, and/or new academic programs. "Both colleges proclaimed their institutions were resetting tuition from a position of strength, not desperation." The two less successful institutions did not have the financial strength or expertise to effectively market their institutional brand and did not have a story of investment and growth to tell. "They could only communicate about price." Their markets responded unfavorably (Casamento 2016, 77).

Just as important was due diligence. A tuition reset is an exercise requiring complex planning. "The decision cannot be rushed. . . . The investment in external pricing and marketing assistance is critical. Only two of the colleges participating in the study utilized outside consultants and they were the only two colleges in the study that experienced an increase in undergraduate tuition revenue in the first year of the tuition price reset implementation" (Casamento 2016, 79).

Finally, the campus leader who would inherit the task of implementing Utica's tuition reset came to understand well the dictum "communicate effectively." Two important pieces of the communications strategy are the training of staff and returning student messaging. "The communications strategy should include the timing of staff training and the detail behind the following questions: 1) what campus groups need to be trained; 2) what do the different campus groups need to know; and 3) when do the different campus groups need to know it?" (Casamento 2016, 83).

The second study by Andrew Armitage (2018), an experienced institutional researcher and self-proclaimed "numbers guy," was undertaken two years later and drew on the success of the Utica College tuition reset and the strength of Casamento's analysis. In a study that combined both statistical analysis and frank interviews with campus leaders and administrators, Armitage asked the same basic questions as Casamento had asked:

What are the tangible benefits experienced by an institution following a tuition reset?

Is a tuition reset sustainable over a period of multiple years?

For his study, Armitage identified 12 private four-year colleges and universities that had implemented a tuition reset, and then tracked their performance for the two years following the reset. How these institutions implemented their tuition resets and their subsequent experiences illustrates just how variable the practice remains and how uncertain are the results. The reduction in sticker price among these 12 private institutions ranged from a low of 8 percent to a high of 43 percent. On average, there was a 25 percent reduction in published sticker prices. But the results were certainly mixed.

To measure the impact of the tuition resets, Armitage developed a set of comparator institutions each paired with one of the 12 institutions that implemented a reset. In the two years prior to the tuition reset, average enrollment at the 12 resetting institutions was on a downward slope. However, average enrollment at the comparator institutions was on a slight upward trend. The reset changed that story. The resetting institutions enjoyed enrollment increases of 12 percent in the year of the reset, 11 percent the next year, and another 4 percent in the last year for which Armitage had data. The comparator institutions headed in the opposite direction: no average increase in the year the other institutions reset their tuitions, a 5 percent increase the following year, and then on average a 10 percent loss in enrollment the final year of the analysis.

Enrollment increases tell only half the story. Institutions resetting their tuitions—that is, institutions reducing their sticker prices and commensurately reducing their discount rates—could hope for one of two possible outcomes: a reduction of the discount rate such that net tuition revenue per student did not decrease or an increase in enrollment to substitute for the loss of tuition dollars occasioned by the lowering of net tuition on a per-student basis. In other words, they might hope to see an increase in volume that could offset a decrease in rate.

While enrollments across the 12 resetting institutions did increase, even substantially at two of the colleges, total tuition income net of institutionally funded student aid (NTR) did not. Or, as Armitage quietly noted:

> The results of the 12 institutions illustrate that, for three quarters of the studied schools, their implementation of a tuition reset was not successful at increasing either total NTR [net tuition revenue] or NTR per

student FTE in the year of the reset. With small, private institutions dependent on tuition revenue to fund operations, these results call into question the impact a tuition reset may have on the financial sustainability of an institution. (Armitage 2018, 21)

In addition to his statistical analysis, Armitage interviewed a host of campus administrators and, in the process, came to understand how and why institutional leaders opted to try a tuition reset. His report of this aspect of the research begins with a story reported to him about what the media were most interested in.

The first question the media asked was, "How can you do this? How can you cut your tuition 43%?" That's where we had to try to explain, "We're not cutting tuition 43%. We're cutting the sticker price, and what we're doing is we're bringing the products closer to the actual cost of education, so that students have a more honest picture of what we're doing, and also so that future tuition increases will be on a lower dollar base." (Armitage 2018, 30)

As Casamento noted, communications are crucial in implementing this strategy, and this is as good an explanation of a tuition reset as one is likely to find.

Most of those Armitage talked with were equally blunt about the perceived risk that a reduction of an institution's sticker price was an early warning of more trouble to come.

What's the worst that can be said about us . . . this must mean they're in trouble. This must mean it's a gimmick, and there's bound to be some fine print in there. So, we said this is a risk we're willing to take. . . . It's simple, it's straightforward, the emphasis in everything that we said and did to roll it out was accessibility and affordability, and it was simple enough. It didn't take three paragraphs to explain it, and you didn't have to read it three times to see if it applied to you. It was real simple, really straightforward. (Armitage 2018, 35)

One final thought from a leader at an institution that stabilized both its undergraduate enrollment and its net tuition per full-time student:

When people talk to me about reset strategies one of the things I always remind them is the first year is actually the easiest. The hardest part of those successes and I see this with those that haven't succeeded is management of that tuition, that revenue over time. (Armitage 2018, 40)

Taken together the Casamento (2016) and Armitage (2018) studies explain why a tuition reset seems like such an exciting idea until the moment of truth arrives. The implementation is necessarily complex, the risks often understated, and a positive result anything but guaranteed. Whatever the risks for the long term may be, this is a strategy that can buy time, perhaps as much as five years. It's possible that being engaged in the issue helps focus a campus's attention on just how perilous the future might be, perhaps paving the way for other, longer-term strategies.

We suspect that in the long run even a fundamental change in pricing policy is not likely to protect those institutions at substantial market risk. The alternative is either to grow one's enrollment by a substantial percentage or reduce instructional expenditures by a similar percentage. Most campus leaders will likely protest that once again we have offered a Hobson's choice—that they have neither the marketing muscle to increase enrollments nor the political capacity to reduce instructional costs.

Which brings us to one of the most asked questions of higher education: *Isn't technology the answer?* There is now a near endless debate as to whether electronic learning modalities can reduce cost, produce the same result as old-fashioned in-class instruction by a real person, and are not dehumanizing in general and counter to the spirit of the humanities and liberal arts in particular. Nor do we have lots of well-documented examples of colleges and universities that substantially reduced their instructional costs through the introduction of electronic instruction to supply a credible answer. What we do have is a pair of stories that suggest the kinds of cost reductions we have in mind are at least possible.

The first of these innovations, Studio Physics, was pioneered by Jack Wilson and his physics colleagues at Rensselaer Polytechnic Institute in the mid-1990s (RPI 2012). It was an innovation that began with a simple observation. The most expensive component of a traditional Physics 101 course were the large lecture sections that most students routinely skipped. Attendance at the weekly discussion sections conducted by the department's tenure-track faculty were often attended by less than half the registered students. Only the labs—which in practice focused just on the problem sets a successful student was expected to master—were regularly attended.

The defining characteristic of Studio Physics was the reliance on computers clustered in large, open learning spaces—the studios of Studio Physics—to deliver most of the instruction. Students worked in pairs on problem sets that constitute the basic Physics 101 curriculum. Detailed simulations of the problems were presented via computer, while a small team of faculty roamed the studio available to answer questions and help students get unstuck. While Studio Physics is still a mode of instruction in a limited number of physics programs today, the mystery that surrounds the innovation is why it has not been picked up by other disciplines.

Our second example is more recent. It tells the story of the University of Central Florida's sustaining investment in online learning as a means of supplementing face-to-face instruction, suggesting in the process that such substitutions may well offer small colleges the best chance of lowering their prices while preserving instructional quality. The University of Central Florida was not facing a significant enrollment shortfall. Quite the contrary, the university was mandated to serve significantly more students without a corresponding augment in state funding. The University of Central Florida is also something of a flawed example—a university that enshrined bigness as a strategic imperative: big football, big research, and big buildings which, it turned out, were financed in awkward ways (Stripling 2019).

That said, what makes the University of Central Florida of interest are the lessons it and its faculty learned about increasing faculty productivity—lessons that smaller institutions trying to reduce instructional costs might well find instructive. Central Florida's story was developed for us by Peggy McCready, like Casamento and Armitage, a graduate of University of Pennsylvania's Executive Doctorate in Higher

Education Management Program. She completed her dissertation in 2013 and, following a stint at the University of Oxford as its director of Academic IT, was appointed Northwestern University's associate vice president of IT Services.

> In 2012, the University of Central Florida was a relatively new institution with big ambitions. Ranked by *U.S. News* as an "up and coming" institution, the university in 2012 had just under 60,000 students making it the second largest university in the United States. At the same time, and not so coincidentally, the University's support from the State of Florida had decreased dramatically, dropping $144,000,000 over the previous five years. The University compensated by developing a "can do culture." As one faculty member told McCready: "The great thing about being part of an institution like UCF is that we can go in whatever direction we think is innovative and cutting edge in order to increase opportunity for our students." A department chair later spelled out what this claim meant in more traditional terms, "While we have traditions, they are not traditions that keep the institution in place. They're traditions that help us move forward." Foremost among those traditions was the University's sense of itself as a "tech heavy" place. (McCready 2013, 39–44)

Among the advantages the University of Central Florida could count on was a demonstrated ability to do more with less. Between 2008 and 2012, the university experienced a 20 percent increase in the size of its undergraduate student body. Over the same period of time, the number of faculty (full-time teaching and adjunct faculty) increased by just 60 positions, or 4.7 percent. In short, the university taught a lot more students while receiving significantly less state funding and almost no increase in faculty positions.

How was this growth plus increased faculty productivity achieved? By an outsized application of technology and the widespread adoption of online courses that came to absorb roughly a third of the course units generated annually by University of Central Florida students. Here McCready drew on an extensive interview with Joel Hartman, then the university's vice provost of Information Technology and Resources. The story Hartman told began with the observation that "the way UCF uses technology to support its teaching mission has become its business model, as opposed to something the university does on the side." As a result, the majority of faculty members at the University of Central Florida taught courses in multiple modalities—web-based, mixed-mode, and face-to-face—the university's nomenclature for its course delivery modes. At the same time, these modalities became a regular part of the undergraduate experience across the university. Hartman summed up his score of how well the faculty and students embraced the university's strategy by noting:

> The course modalities have become so embedded into the University's culture that everyone speaks in terms of modality labels—the W's, the M's, and so forth—which have become part of the institution's vocabulary. . . . As far as student preferences in course delivery, the web-based courses tend to fill up first, followed by mixed-mode and then face-to-face courses. In fact, many of the students living on campus are taking web-based and mixed-mode courses, suggesting that student choice is a matter of convenience and personal learning preference, as opposed to strictly an issue of access. While students can complete most degree programs without taking any on-line courses, it's rare for a student to get through their entire program without taking an on-line class. (McCready 2013, 46)

The University of Central Florida proved that it is possible to change how an undergraduate curriculum is delivered. It could do so because its faculty embraced growth through technology and accepted a strategy requiring a substantial increase in faculty productivity as measured by a decreasing faculty-to-student ratio. For its part, the university offered extraordinary incentives that recognized faculty members who taught beyond the median class size, which could only be achieved through the delivery of online courses. Annual, onetime teaching awards of $2,000 were awarded to up to 50 faculty members. Faculty who taught more than the median class size in their department could receive a permanent boost in pay of $5,000. No less, it was a strategy fueled by an extraordinary growth in student numbers, not a decline. The lesson is that changing higher education's business model is within the realm of the possible. And it requires taking advantage of a mode of education that has a lower overhead cost than a traditional residential college experience.

To state what is undoubtedly obvious to institutional leaders, this kind of change isn't easy. Setting aside the challenges of selling this kind of change to a campus community, few of the 7 percent of institutions already at the highest substantial market risk—that is, with scores of 6 or higher—have the capital necessary to front-end the investment in the electronic modalities the strategy requires. Even fewer can expect the kind of growth in student numbers that allowed the University of Central Florida to reduce unit costs by 20 percent without a commensurate reduction in faculty and related instructional support staff. The growing array of for-profit Online Program Management (OPM) companies that provide institutions with everything from short-term support and capacity-building services to full-service partnerships (with commensurate revenue sharing) is evidence that at least some colleges and universities are recognizing both the opportunities and the challenges of launching such an initiative (Czerniewicz and Walji 2019). However schools go about developing and delivering these programs intended to generate new revenue, there is no question that an initial, sometimes significant, investment is required. It would be easier if a number of the large foundations that argue for increased completions and lower collegiate prices provided some of the requisite start-up funding. One can always wish.

An Alternate Path

For most institutions experiencing substantial risk, there is an alternate path—one that boosts total enrollments by increasing the rate of freshman-sophomore retention. The median freshman-to-sophomore retention rate for Four-Year Public institutions in 2016 was 75.5 percent, which means that half the institutions were losing nearly a quarter of their freshman class in their first year. Ten percent of the Four-Year Public institutions lost more than a third of their freshmen. The numbers for Four-Year Private Not-for-Profit institutions are not much better. The median freshman-to-sophomore retention rate was 77.6 percent and at the 10th percentile the retention rate was 56 percent.

Improving college completion rates has become a national goal, spawning in the process a host of nostrums for increasing the number of college students who persist. Most focus on improving student support services and expect little of the faculty beyond staying on message. There are, however, exceptions. Beverly Tatum, former president of Spelman College, makes clear that success in educating students means connecting with them in meaningful ways—the students who stay the course are those who believe they belong. Fostering that sense of "I belong here" is a necessary condition for succeeding with all students, at-risk students in particular. Byron White in an often-angry essay in *Inside Higher Ed* pushed the argument further:

> The slogan that to succeed students in college needed to be "college ready," he wrote, was a paradigm that has allowed higher education to deflect accountability. It is time that we fully embrace the burden of being student-ready institutions. After all, not only is the notion of college ready an excuse, but new practices in student success have exposed it as something of a farce. It turns out the problem was not as much about the students as we thought. It was largely us, uninformed about what it takes to help them succeed or unwilling to allocate the resources necessary to put it into practice. (White 2016)

In a private email exchange, he also wanted us to take note of the new Honors College at Rutgers University–Newark:

> After finding that every honors program in the country was biased toward white, affluent students—even as they professed to desire greater diversity—Rutgers dismissed the notion that affluent white kids were fundamentally more worthy of merit and rejected the assessment of "honors" that inevitably tilted in their favor. When they "suspended the rules and rethought the problem," as you implored us to do, they ended up with an honors college where two-thirds of the students who qualify are residents of Newark. Oh, and by the way, black and white students

at Rutgers-Newark graduate at the exact same rate, which is higher than the national average. (Byron White, personal communication)

We are about to argue that the rules that need to be revisited involve much more than who is "college ready" and hence worthy of admission. We have suspected for some time that the problem may be as basic as the college curriculum students experience when they begin their collegiate studies. Most often the curriculum is conceived as a sort of funnel: students start with broader "general education" courses, and eventually come to specialize in a major area of study. And for many, a good general education is understood to be the hallmark of a truly liberal education. Students are encouraged to explore a wide range of topics to provide a broad intellectual context for their more specialized future major. Most efforts aimed at reforming general education have sought to strengthen its commitment to intellectual exploration and, not incidentally, to lessen the degree to which the general education curriculum serves as an academic bazaar in which faculty, particularly from underenrolled departments, recruit new majors.

Our explorations began with an extended analysis of a successful effort to recast the general education requirements at the University of Wisconsin Oshkosh. Once a proposed revision of the gen-ed requirements was in hand, a survey asked all interested undergraduates to comment on both the new and old sets of requirements. Here *Checklist for Change* picks up the story:

> Most of the three hundred-plus who responded to the survey had little understanding of what was being proposed, but they knew exactly what was wrong with the general education requirements to which they had been subjected. Just half of those who responded said that general education at Oshkosh was a "valuable component." Even fewer said that the general education curriculum provided a "foundation for success in my major." Perhaps in the unkindest cut of all, less than half agreed with the statement that the University's general education requirements were "clearly understood and explained by academic advisers across campus."
>
> The most specific as well as most repeated comment . . . was that the general education curriculum was "a waste of time and money." The

second most common complaint was that the general education require-
ment "is very disorganized and does not link to a major." Some of the
students' comments were wonderfully prescient in their estimate of the
faculty's commitment to a well-formed introduction to the liberal arts.
As one student put it, too much of general education at Oshkosh does
nothing "more than keep particularly irrelevant courses funded and tired
faculty continually employed." (Zemsky 2013, 148–149)

In the years since, we have concluded that a national survey of undergraduates would largely replicate the Oshkosh survey finding that half
of students reported: the gen-ed curriculum was a waste of time and
money. We are aware that most faculty would likely disagree. And, of
course, even half the students at Oshkosh felt that the general education
courses had value. Our concern here, however, is with the other half—
those students who start the college experience needing to be convinced
about the value of their education, with their bags metaphorically never
unpacked. What we know about many of these students is that general
education is not what they want, and, at many institutions, a third or
more of them will not be around to start their sophomore year.

We have started asking a simple set of questions: What would be
the freshman-to-sophomore retention rate if the students' first year
was explicitly tied to the students' interests, which are increasingly
vocational? Could they start with a true introduction to their preferred
major? Could the first-year focus on practical learning skills that have
a postgraduation payoff in the labor market: writing, statistics, problem solving, and, yes, a foreign language? Here we need to be clear—
we are not talking about general education courses that have each of
these skills as subthemes. Nor are we arguing for abandoning the kind
of intellectual growth a really good gen-ed curriculum promises. Our
alternative, as one of the institutions now considering our proposal
labeled it, is to "flip the curriculum." Start practical and skill centered
but insist that no one graduates without spending a good portion of
their junior and senior years engaged in a broad, probably self-designed
exploration of topics outside but ideally connected in meaningful ways
to their majors.

We also know that such a proposal requires as fulsome a change in faculty behaviors as does our proposal for a curriculum that blends in-face and electronic learning modalities. Only a faculty can design and deliver the kind of first-year, skill-based vocationally tinged experience we have in mind. And that is the principal lesson our ruminations about the link between attrition and curriculum has taught us. The kind of improvement in an institution's freshman-to-sophomore retention, which institutions at market risk require, will inevitably entail a rethinking of the curriculum in general and the first-year experience in particular. Only the faculty, not as individuals nor individual departments, but collectively, can produce the kind of changes that retaining more students requires.

More Than the Numbers

We promised at the outset that our exploration of market stress would be about more than just the numbers. The best way to honor that promise is to offer a set of practical, albeit difficult, strategies for institutions to counter the market forces accounting for their negative Market Stress Test Scores. Those strategies we have now presented: consider a tuition reset in order to buy some time; seek a large—perhaps 20 percent or more—reduction in market price by reducing instructional costs an equal amount; or reengineer the first-year curriculum to reduce freshman-to-sophomore attrition by making the institution more student ready.

We want to conclude by exploring how two institutions are responding to the market pressures the Market Stress Test Scores reflect. Both institutions were among the four we asked to think about our analysis and whether it fit. The first was Utica College in Central New York. The Utica College Stress Test exemplifies the capacity of a Market Stress Test Score to illustrate a story worth telling (figure 7.1). Through 2014, the college's intake of first-time first-year students was on a downward slope, which the college's tuition reset in 2015 reversed.

Retention of freshman-to-sophomore status improved, but at 75 percent, there remained room for significant improvement. The

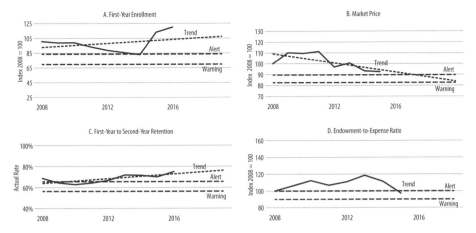

Figure 7.1. Components of Market Stress Test for Utica College.

most troublesome indicator was market price, which through 2016 had yet to stabilize, suggesting that further price reductions might be in order. The 2016 ratio of the endowment to expenditure is a reflection of the trouble Utica College was having in funding its discount rate.

In January 2019, Karen Vahey, another student in the University of Pennsylvania's Executive Doctorate in Higher Education Management Program, interviewed Jeff Gates, senior vice president for Student Life and Enrollment Management at Utica College. Gates was new to the college and represented a shift in the kind of leaders the college was looking for. What he brought to the job was wide experience working for public institutions in New York State and an appetite for data analysis.

Vahey's telling of Gates's story continues from there. The first step was to conduct a pricing study that asked

> prospective students and their families . . . about the optimal price they
> wanted to pay. In other words, did they prefer a high price tag with a
> high discount through scholarships and grants or a tuition reset model?
> The results of the study suggested that, simply put, families just wanted
> to pay less. Utica moved forward with a tuition reset though they no
> longer refer to it as a reset—"this is just our cost."

The goal of the tuition reset was two-fold. First, the College wanted "to prevent sticker shock and stop families from walking away from a private education." And the market responded. Applications [have] increased by 15% since the reset. And the population itself changed. Families with greater income have been considering Utica in greater numbers. As a result, the net tuition grew from approximately $13,000 per student in 2015 to its current $17,000. The second goal of the reset was to save students money over time and it will save students approximately 20%—lowering both out of pocket expenses and loan borrowing amounts. (Vahey 2019)

The process has abounded with benefits to Utica College, not the least of which was the campus finally coming to terms with its actual competition. When asked who were Utica's principal competitors, faculty and staff most often responded with the names of private, highly selective Medallions such as Hamilton College and Colgate University. Gates followed up with analysis of FAFSA (Free Application for Federal Student Aid) data and then told the community that 7 of Utica's top 10 competitors were New York State public colleges and universities. Convincing the faculty in particular of this alternate reality, Gates later told Vahey, "wasn't easy. They didn't want to believe it at first until they really understood . . . the data . . . we were showing them" (Vahey 2019).

Utica College's tuition reset is also a prime example of Armitage's observation (2018) that resets worked best when they were part of a larger set of strategic initiatives. The college is simultaneously expanding its graduate education program through online and hybrid offerings and exploring opening a branch of its nursing programs in a state where there is demand but a dearth of nursing programs. Its most interesting new direction from our perspective is a discussion initiated by the president of the possibility of a renewed focus on retention anchored by a flipping of the college's gen-ed programs. As the president told us, time will tell.

Our second example of a Market Stress Test Score that has engendered a reconsideration of both strategy and practice is Central College

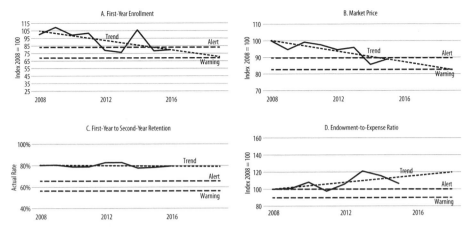

Figure 7.2. Components of Market Stress Test for Central College.

in Iowa (figure 7.2). Its president, Mark Putnam, is a well-regarded student of higher education, who, before coming to Central was a key member of Richard Freeland's team at Northeastern University, responsible for the major repositioning of that university. Central's Market Stress Test Score tells the story of a well-established institution facing mounting difficulties recruiting first-year classes of sufficient size to maintain its standing in the Midwest's turbulent higher education market.

For Central, recruiting a freshman class had become an increasingly puzzling operation. Having invested heavily in market research, the college believed it had turned the corner in 2014 when that year's freshman class suddenly returned to pre-2010 levels. Thereafter, however, the freshman enrollments resumed their downward slope. Analytically, nothing seemed to make sense until 2017 when the college engaged in a second round of market studies, this time focusing on prices and shifts in the Iowa market.

At this point, Putnam began a yearlong rethinking as to what he might ask of his college. By the fall of 2018, he was ready with an answer, which he shared first with his board and subsequently with his campus community. His paper—"A Meta-strategy for the Future of Central College"—is a rich statement from an accomplished analyst as well as college president describing what it means to be at substantial risk. His narrative begins more than a little wistfully:

> For me it has been a stimulating journey that has stretched my professional knowledge and tested my personal resolve. There have been days of incredible despair and days of immense enthusiasm. It has been an endless exercise in revision in which I have discarded far more than I have retained. As I contemplate the future I am more persuaded than ever that the experience of the past will not be the experience of the future. We are clearly in a period of systemic transition and I am convinced that the role Central College can and should play in the future higher education landscape is different than conventional wisdom would dictate.

He understood well that past strategies for fixing the problem will likely prove inadequate—that proceeding in the future as in the past would not work:

> Sometimes the simplest answers are simply wrong, though on the surface they seem logical and rooted in common sense. Among others, futurists have reminded us that we tend to overestimate short-term trends and underestimate long-term trends. So the risk of misguided choices is found in clinging to simple operational solutions set in the context of short-term thinking. That type of change management only amplifies this problem as the sense of urgency overtakes the more fundamental importance of strategic direction.

Then he puts the problem squarely before his community:

> The traditional notion of a church-affiliated, residential, liberal arts college has lost its rhetorical relevance in American society. Interestingly, the underlying experience represented in those kinds of descriptors remain highly desirable to many, but the ways in which we have embodied and articulated those characteristics lack coherence in today's marketplace for students and parents.

There are no villains, he tells his colleagues, but rather a "six-pack of change," including

1) Demographic Decline
2) Economic Uncertainty
3) Workforce Expectations
4) Technological Innovation
5) Societal Change
6) Public Policy

The consequence is now a price war among the midwestern colleges with which Central competes for new students. As a consequence, we have suffered at the hands of our peer institutions in our immediate market, that have discounted more heavily, some against higher sticker prices. There is even evidence in the research that tells us there is a greater sensitivity to the dollar value of the discount offered rather than the net price. However, I continue to maintain that we cannot cut, borrow, and discount our way to success. We have to find another way. Incremental changes in our recruiting operation will not address the depth of the problem we are facing. Pricing tactics in the face of aggressive price competition will not have a stabilizing effect and will only mask a fundamental lack of perceived quality. The challenge is further exacerbated by a stunning lack of visibility for Central College in the broader marketplace. (Putnam 2018)

No one in our experience has said it better than Putnam.

Saying it better, however, is not the answer. What Putnam and his senior leadership team have proposed is but a beginning. First, a modest tuition reset to buy some time and some understanding on the part of the board to allow the application of extraordinary funds in the short term. Simultaneously, the college will launch the much-needed discussion of mission—one that both draws on Central's traditional assets and incorporates a firmer sense of what students and their parents really want and are ready to pay for. Thereafter comes an equally tough revision of the college's curriculum, one that speaks to the college's traditional values and, at the same time, provides instructional pathways that exemplify a student-ready institution.

The importance of the Utica and Central reactions to their shifting market circumstances verifies the principal vectors we have placed at the core of our analysis: freshman recruitment, market price, and freshman-to-sophomore retention. Each institution understands well that changes in the curriculum will likely prove necessary and that only a faculty fully engaged in the change process will likely design and implement what is necessary. Neither of these institutions is thinking about a wholesale adoption of e-learning modalities, though in time we suspect they will conclude that a curriculum that blends face-to-face instruction with e-learning modalities offers sufficient advantages to be worth the political struggles that would likely ensue.

Those on the edge of the bubble know there are but a limited number of bright spots anywhere. Matthew Derr, the president of Sterling College in Vermont, commenting on a neighbor and rival's likely demise, made that point and in the process summed up much of what this book has been about:

> I think institutions that are thinking about the closure of competitors as their solution are being pretty shortsighted about the real demographic shift that's coming. . . . There are serious structural challenges and issues that small rural liberal arts colleges are going to face, and just contraction is not going to be enough. (Seltzer 2019)

So, which institutions are likely to close? Not the Medallions or Name Brands, which will likely substitute increased enrollments for increased prices. Nor will institutions like Utica and Central disappear, though they will struggle. Public institutions that face further reductions in public funding will likely be in real trouble. As will be the roughly 7 percent of the nation's colleges and universities already facing substantial risk.

Is It Closing Time?

We are back where we started with a reminder that predicting collegiate closures is a media parlor game that helps neither students nor institutions. What is needed instead is a full and frank discussion rooted in the facts of the matter. The place to start is with a better, more nuanced understanding of the market for an undergraduate education.

Not-for-profit colleges and universities are not businesses, but they are enterprises subject to the shifting currents of a crowded market whose contours are proving increasingly troublesome.

The focus of the discussion we have in mind needs to be on higher education's value proposition, on the one hand, and on the risks the market imposes on institutions in pursuit of their missions, on the other. Market risk is related to but still distinct from the financial risk that has been the focus of most higher education management for more than a decade now. Financial risk means running out of money. Market risk in much the same way means running out of students and first-time first-year (freshman) students in particular. Just as in managing financial risk institutions need to keep track of a relatively few key indicators, managing market risk means keeping track of an equally well-defined set of indicators and whether or not they have been declining over time: new student enrollments, net cash price, retentions to graduation. In this study, we have sought an understanding of market risk in order to gauge how many institutions are likely asking, *Is it closing time?* The answer, we suggest, is that closings will not be nearly as prevalent as many prognosticators have promised and will in fact impact relatively few students. What the numbers tell us is that just 10 percent or less of the nation's colleges and universities face substantial market risk. Sixty percent face little or no market risk. But the remaining 30 percent are institutions that are bound to struggle. To thrive, they will need to reconsider the curricula they deliver, the prices they charge, and their willingness to experiment with new modes of instruction. At the same time, we caution that failing to pay attention to higher education's increasingly muddled value proposition will yield both institutions at risk and a market that makes increasingly less sense to a public already skeptical of higher education's core values.

Risk Index Workbook for Institutional Analysts

Now that you have been introduced to the Market Stress Test Score you may ask, "How can we apply the methodology to understand whether our institution is at risk?" Part of the answer lies in chapter 3, where schematics and examples are presented. A more complete answer will be discussed here.

To replicate the approach described in this book, it is important to use the same variables—that is, the specific IPEDS (Integrated Postsecondary Education Data System) defined variables, albeit updated to reflect current experiences—that were used in the original analysis. It is important, as well, to choose an appropriate time frame for calculating percentage change over time and for fitting a trend line to obtain predictions for future years. Since Excel is widely used, the templates in this appendix are in Excel, show Excel formulas, and provide an efficient way to compute the Market Stress Test Score. Clearly, any spreadsheet program, statistical package, or computational method that allows you to derive the required elements may be employed.

Despite the seeming complexity of the process, there is a marked-out path from beginning to end.

- First, you'll chart your data, and we'll show you how to do that.
- Next, you will be walked through the process for calculating your component scores that determine Market Stress Test Score.
- The third step has you comparing your component scores to the cutoffs we used in the text, recognizing that our values were based on data from the period 2008–2016. (If your analysis time frame is more recent, the distribution of sector-wide data may have shifted.)

As was discussed earlier, the components selected for the Market Stress Test Score are specific for each sector: Four-Year Public, Four-Year Private Not-for-Profit, and Two-Year Public. Thus, there will follow separate presentations of variables and worksheets for institutions in each sector to use. The Four-Year Private Not-for Profit instructions begin on page 122, Four-Year Public follows on page 128, and Two-Year Public can be found beginning on page 133. First, however, we begin with the general principles that will apply to all sectors.

A Time Frame and General Approach for Analysis

The time frame for the analysis presented in chapter 3 was constrained by the availability of IPEDS' public information. The last full year of accessible data for the analysis presented in this volume was either 2016 or 2015, depending on the variable of interest. The first year extracted, or base year, 2008, is one used in the research underpinning *The Market Imperative* (Zemsky and Shaman 2017) and is one in which the IPEDS data definitions were identical to or were compatible with the final year. For your analysis, select the most recent year for which you have institutional data that complies with IPEDS definitions. For example, the retention rate was calculated using cohort and cohort survival counts that met the IPEDS definition of "Full-Time Adjusted Fall 2015 Cohort (EF2016D)" and "Students from the Full-Time Adjusted Fall 2015 Cohort Enrolled in Fall 2016 (EF2016D)." As you update to 2019 and beyond, compute the retention component using the cohort and cohort survival numbers you would submit, or have submitted, to IPEDS for the latest year under study.

The Market Stress Test Score uses an eight-year period for the "change over time" computation and then provides a projection three years out. Select your most recent year and then obtain your IPEDS submissions for the seven prior years. From these data, you can compute a percent change from the base year to the present year and you can construct a trend line—a simple linear fit—from which you can project three years into the future. Each component will be compared to alert and warning thresholds values to obtain a score.

Some components are straightforward in that they are simply numbers reported to IPEDS. Others are more complicated because they require combining several reported numbers that may be provided to IPEDS in different submissions. Dollar figures (excepting those used in ratios) must be converted to real or constant base year dollars. Ultimately, however, the score for each component will be determined by filling in the grid shown in table A.1 with the appropriate variables.

In table A.1, the area from A to B indicates the eight years of data derived from IPEDS variables. From these data C, the percentage change

Table A.1. General method for computing component score for a single factor

A							B	C	D	E	F	G	H	J
Base year	Year 2	Year 3	Year 4	Year 5	Year 6	Year 7	Current or last available year	Percent change current year vs. base year	Projected value 3 years later	Percent change projected 3 years later vs. base year	Percent change C reaches or falls below alert value	Percent change C reaches or falls below warning value	Percent change E reaches or falls below alert value	Risk score
Component IPEDS data	IPEDS data	IPEDS data	IPEDS data	IPEDS data	IPEDS data	IPEDS data	Data submitted to or complying with IPEDS definitions	$(B-A)/A$	From trend line of data for years A through B	$(D-A)/A$	YES=1	YES=1	YES=1	$F+G+H$

IPEDS = Integrated Postsecondary Education Data System.

over the period, is computed. A simple linear fit of the data will allow you to find D, a projected value of the component three years hence, and to compute E, the change in the component from the base year to the projected year. C and E are then compared to alert and warning values.

Four-Year Private Not-for-Profit Market Stress Test Score Computation

The four factors for assessing stress, that is, for producing the Market Stress Test Score for a Four-Year Private Not-for-Profit institution include two that are straightforward and two that require computation. The enrollment components—first-year degree-seeking undergraduates and retention—are the easiest to reproduce and need only an IPEDS reference. Creating the more complex market price and endowment-to-expense ratio, described next, requires more work. Later in this section tables A.3 to A.5 provide directions to the specific IPEDS variables and any special computation needed to produce the components.

After you have chosen the time frame for calculating risk, you may wish to set up a worksheet or a spreadsheet that resembles the template in table A.2. The data entered into table A.2 covers an eight-year period with the earliest year labeled "base year" and the last year labeled "most recent year." The four components are shown in columns C to F, row 1.

The data in column C, rows 2 through 9 are the first-year enrollments for the fall of each year. As is specified in table A.3, which illustrates the source of the variable for a sample year, the IPEDS definition for this column is the first-year degree-seeking undergraduates. The data section of column D is populated with the first- to second-year retention rate as described in table A.3.

Turning to column E, market price is computed by subtracting the average institutional grant to first-year full-time students from the stated tuition and fees. Once that is determined, a GDP (gross domestic product) deflator must be applied to cast the price for each year in constant (real) base year dollars. A good source for the GDP deflator is https://fred .stlouisfed.org/series/GDPDEF since it has quarterly values. It is convenient to set the base year to 100 and then to determine the relative GDP deflator for subsequent years. The IPEDS sources for the construction of this variable are displayed in table A.4.

Finally, the data for column F are obtained by dividing the year-end value of your institution's endowment by the total expenses for that year. If there is a hospital associated with your institution, you need to subtract the hospital expense. Table A.5 presents the IPEDS variables for a sample year.

Table A.2. Worksheet for Four-Year Private Not-for-Profit institutions

		Excel column				
	A	B	C	D	E Market price in constant base year dollars	F
	Counter	Year	First year	Retention		Endowment/expenses
Excel Row 1						
Data zone						
2	1	Base year = Year 1	N	%	$	Ratio
3	2	Year 2	N	%	$	Ratio
4	3	Year 3	N	%	$	Ratio
5	4	Year 4	N	%	$	Ratio
6	5	Year 5	N	%	$	Ratio
7	6	Year 6	N	%	$	Ratio
8	7	Year 7	N	%	$	Ratio
9	8	Most recent year = Year 8	N	%	$	Ratio
Computation zone						
10		% change recent vs. base	=(C9-C2)/C2	=(D9-D2)/D2	=(E9-E2)/E2	=(F9-F2)/F2
11		Slope of line	=SLOPE(C2:C9, A2:A9)	=SLOPE (D2:D9, A2:A9)	=SLOPE(E2:E9, A2:A9)	=SLOPE(F2:F9, A2:A9)
12		Intercept of line	=INTERCEPT (C2:C9, A2:A9)	=INTERCEPT (D2:D9, A2:A9)	=INTERCEPT (E2:E9, A2:A9)	=INTERCEPT (F2:F9, A2:A9)
13		Projected value most recent year + 3	C12+(11*C11)	D12+(11*D11)	E12+(11*E11)	F12+(11*F11)
14		% change projected year vs. base year	=(C13-C2)/C2	=(D13-D2)/D2	=(E13-E2)/E2	=(F13-F2)/F2

Table A.2. (Continued)

	Excel Row	A — Counter	B — Year	C — First year	D — Retention	E — Market price in constant base year dollars	F — Endowment/expenses
Testing zone	15		% change recent year vs. base year reaches or falls below alert value	=if(C10<=C18,1,0)	=if(D10<=D18,1,0)	=if(E10<=E18,1,0)	=if(F10<=F18,1,0)
	16		% change recent year vs. base year reaches or falls below warning value	=if(C10<=C19,1,0)	=if(D10<=D19,1,0)	=if(E10<=E19,1,0)	=if(F10<=F19,1,0)
	17		% change projected year vs. base year reaches or falls below alert value	=if(C14<=C18,1,0)	=if(D14<=D18,1,0)	=if(E14<=E18,1,0)	=if(F14<=F18,1,0)
Thresholds	18		Alert value	17.4%	65.6%	-10.4%	0.0%
	19		Warning value	30.8%	56.4%	-17.5%	-10.3%
Results	20		Component score	=C15+C16+C17	=D15+D16+D17	=E15+E16+E17	=F15+F16+F17
	21		Total Market Stress Test Score				=C20+D20+E20+F20

Table A.3. Four-Year Private Not-for-Profit institutions IPEDS variables and formulas for computing "risk" scores for first year and retention

Component	IPEDS variable	Component variable	IPEDS category		Subcategories	
First year	Grand total (EF2016, all students undergraduate degree-/certificate-seeking first-time)	Change over time using IPEDS variable	Fall enrollment	Gender, attendance status, and level of student	Fall 1984 to current year	Gender, attendance status, and level of student	Level of student, undergraduate, degree-/certificate-seeking: total; first-time: grand total
Retention						
A	Full-time adjusted fall 2015 cohort (EF2016D)	Retention rate: B/A in latest year	Retention rates, entering class and student-to-faculty ratio	Retention rates	Fall 2003 to current year	Full-time adjusted fall cohort from prior year	Students from prior year's adjusted full-time fall cohort enrolled in current year
B	Students from the full-time adjusted fall 2015 cohort enrolled in fall 2016 (EF2016D)					

Note: Years shown, e.g., EF2016, are examples. IPEDS = Integrated Postsecondary Education Data System.

Table A.4. Four-Year Private Not-for-Profit institutions IPEDS variables and formulas for computing scores for market price

Component	IPEDS variable	Constant dollars	Component variable	IPEDS category	Subcategories			
Market price								
A	Published in-state tuition and fees 2016–2017 (IC2016_AY)	Real market price = (A−(C/B)) / GDP deflator fall 2016 × 100	Change over time of real market price	Student charges	Price of attendance for full-time, first-time undergraduate students (academic year programs)	Tuition and fees: 2006–2007 to current year		Published in-state tuition (current year)
B	Full-time total (EF2015 all students, undergraduate degree-/certificate-seeking first-time)			Fall enrollment	Gender, attendance status, and level of student	Fall 1984 to current year	Gender, attendance status, and level of student	Level of student, undergraduate: degree-/certificate-seeking total: first-time, full-time
C	Total amount of institutional grant aid awarded to full-time first-time undergraduates (SFA1516)			Student financial aid and net price	Student financial aid	1998–1999 to current year	Financial aid to full-time, first-time degree-/certificate-seeking under-graduate students	Total amount of institutional grant aid awarded to full-time first-time undergraduates

Note: Years shown, e.g., IC2016_AY, are examples. IPEDS = Integrated Postsecondary Education Data System.

Table A.5. Four-Year Private Not-for-Profit institutions IPEDS variables and formulas for computing scores for endowment-to-expenses ratio

		IPEDS variable	Component variable	IPEDS category	Subcategories			
Endowment / Expenses	A	Value of endowment assets at the end of the fiscal year (F1516_F2)	Change over time of endowment to expenses A/B or A/(B − C) where applicable	Finance	Private not-for-profit institutions or public institutions using FASB		Endowment assets 2003 to present	Value of endowment assets year-end (current year)
	B	Total expenses - Total amount (F1516_F2)		Finance	Expenses by functional and natural classification: fiscal years 1997 to 2015/ expenses and salaries and wages by function and total expenses by natural classification: Fiscal years 2016 to current year	Total expenses- Total amount	FY 1997 to 2015 /2016 to current	Total expenses-Total amount
	C	Hospital services- Total amount (F1516_F2)—if institution has associated hospitals				Hospital services- Total amount	FY 1997 to 2015 / 2016 to current	Hospital services-Total amount

Note: Years shown, e.g., F1516_F2, are examples. FASB = Financial Accounting Standards Board; IPEDS = Integrated Postsecondary Education Data System.

Once all the data are obtained and these data, plus the threshold values, which are provided in rows 18 and 19 of the table A.2 template, are entered into the worksheet, then a series of calculations—shown here as Excel formulas—must be completed. The component subscores are derived in rows 15 to 17, the total score for each component in row 20, and finally, F21 displays the Market Stress Test Score for your institution.

Four-Year Public Market Risk Test Score Computation

The four components for assessing stress, that is, for producing the Market Stress Test Score for a Four-Year Public institution include three that are relatively straightforward and one that requires computation. The enrollment components, first-year, degree-seeking undergraduates and retention, are the easiest to reproduce and need only an IPEDS reference. The state appropriation values are those directly reported to IPEDS, but for the risk analysis a GDP deflator is applied to cast the values in constant base year dollars. To compute market price, you must take into account the different in-state and out-of-state tuition levels and the proportion of in-state and out-of-state first-year, full-time, degree-seeking undergraduates who enter your institution each fall. Later in this section, tables A.7 and A.8 provide directions to the specific IPEDS variables and any special computation needed to produce the components.

After you have chosen the time frame for calculating risk, you may wish to set up a worksheet or spreadsheet that resembles the template in table A.6. The data entered into table A.6 covers an eight-year period with the earliest year labeled "Base Year" and the last year labeled "Most Recent Year." The four components are shown in columns C to F, row 1.

Once all the data are obtained and these data, plus the threshold values, which are provided in rows 18 and 19 of the table A.6 template, are entered into the worksheet, then a series of calculations—shown here as Excel formulas—must be completed. The component subscores are derived in rows 15 to 17, the total score for each component in row 20, and finally, F21 displays the Market Stress Test Score for your institution.

Turning to column E, the data here are obtained directly from your IPEDS submission. However, the annual value of the appropriation needs to be converted to real, that is, constant base year dollars. A good source for the GDP deflator is https://fred.stlouisfed.org/series/GDPDEF since it

Table A.6. Worksheet for Four-Year Public institutions

	Excel Row	A	B	C	D	E	F
		Counter	Year	First year	Retention	State appropriations in constant base year dollars	Market price in constant base year dollars
Data zone	2	1	Base year = Year 1	N	%	$	$
	3	2	Year 2	N	%	$	$
	4	3	Year 3	N	%	$	$
	5	4	Year 4	N	%	$	$
	6	5	Year 5	N	%	$	$
	7	6	Year 6	N	%	$	$
	8	7	Year 7	N	%	$	$
	9	8	Most recent year = Year 8	N	%	$	$
Computation zone	10		% change recent vs. base	=(C9-C2)/C2	=(D9-D2)/D2	=(E9-E2)/E2	=(F9-F2)/F2
	11		Slope of line	=SLOPE(C2:C9, A2:A9)	=SLOPE (D2:D9, A2:A9)	=SLOPE (E2:E9, A2:A9)	=SLOPE(F2:F9, A2:A9)
	12		Intercept of line	=INTERCEPT (C2:C9, A2:A9)	=INTERCEPT (D2:D9, A2:A9)	=INTERCEPT (E2:E9, A2:A9)	=INTERCEPT (F2:F9, A2:A9)
	13		Projected value most recent year + 3	C12+(11*C11)	D12+(11*D11)	E12+(11*E11)	F12+(11*F11)
	14		% change projected year vs. base year	=(C13-C2)/C2	=(D13-D2)/D2	=(E13-E2)/E2	=(F13-F2)/F2
Testing zone	15		% change recent year vs. base year reaches or falls below alert value	=if(C10<=C18,1,0)	=if(D10<=D18,1,0)	=if(E10<=E18,1,0)	=if(F10<=F18,1,0)
	16		% change recent year vs. base year reaches or falls below warning value	=if(C10<=C19,1,0)	=if(D10<=D19,1,0)	=if(E10<=E19,1,0)	=if(F10<=F19,1,0)
	17		% change projected year vs. base year reaches or falls below alert value	=if(C14<=C18,1,0)	=if(D14<=D18,1,0)	=if(E14<=E18,1,0)	=if(F14<=F18,1,0)
Thresholds	18		Alert value (%)	-15.4%	68%	-27%	0.0%
	19		Warning value (%)	-25.6%	62%	-37%	-8.3%
Results	20		Components	=C15+C16+C17	=D15+D16+D17	=E15+E16+E17	=F15+F16+F17
	21		Total Market Stress Test Score				=C20+D20+E20+F20

Table A.7. Four-Year Public institutions IPEDS variables and formulas for computing scores for first year, retention, and appropriations

Component		IPEDS variable	Component variable	IPEDS category	Subcategories			
First year		Grand total (EF2016 all students under-graduate degree-/certificate-seeking first-time)	Change over time using IPEDS variable	Fall enrollment	Gender, attendance status, and level of student	Fall 1984 to current year	Gender, attendance status, and level of student	Level of student: undergraduate, degree-/certificate-seeking total, first-time, grand total
Retention	A	Full-time adjusted fall 2015 cohort (EF2016D)	Retention rate: B/A in latest year	Retention rates, entering class, and student-to-faculty ratio	Retention rates	Fall 2003 to current year	Full-time adjusted fall cohort from prior year	Students from prior year's adjusted full-time fall cohort enrolled in current year
	B	Students from the full-time adjusted fall 2015 cohort enrolled in fall 2016 (EF2016D)						
State appropriation	C	State appropria-tions (F1516_F1A)	Change over time using IPEDS variable after applying GDP deflator : C /deflator x 100	Finance	Public institutions-GASB 34/35	FY 2002 to current year	Revenues and other additions	State appropriation

Note: Years shown, e.g., EF2016, are examples. IPEDS = Integrated Postsecondary Education Data System.

Table A.8. Four-Year Public institutions IPEDS variables and formulas for computing scores for market price

Component		IPEDS variable	Intermediate computation	Constant dollars	Component variable	IPEDS category	Subcategories		
Market price	A	Published in-state tuition and fees 2015–2016 (IC2015_AY)	X: Average tuition first year ((C / D) × A + (1 − (C / D)) × B	Real market price = (X-Y) / GDP deflator fall 2016 × 100	Change over time of real market price	Student charges	Price of attendance for full-time, first-time undergraduate students (academic year programs)	Tuition and fees: 2006–2007 to current year	Published in-state tuition (current year)
	B	Published out-of-state tuition and fees 2015–2016 (IC2015_AY)				Student charges	Price of attendance for full-time, first-time undergraduate students (academic year programs)	Tuition and fees: 2006–2007 to current year	Published out-of-state tuition (current year)
	C	First-time degree-/certificate-seeking undergraduate students (EF2015C YOUR STATE)				Fall enrollment	Residence and migration of first-time freshmen	First-time degree-/certificate-seeking undergraduate students	Reported number of first-time residents of YOUR state
	D	First-time degree-/certificate-seeking undergraduate students (EF2015C TOTAL)				Fall enrollment	Residence and migration of first-time freshmen	First-time degree-/certificate-seeking undergraduate students	Reported number of first-time TOTAL

Table A.8. (Continued)

Component	IPEDS variable	Intermediate computation	Constant dollars	Component variable	IPEDS category	Subcategories			
E	Full-time total (EF2015 all students undergraduate degree-/certificate-seeking first-time)	Y: Average institutional grant aid to full-time first-time F / E			Fall enrollment	Gender, attendance status, and level of student	Fall 1984 to current year	Gender, attendance status, and level of student	Level of student: undergraduate: degree-/certificate-seeking total: first-time: full-time
F	Total amount of institutional grant aid awarded to full-time first-time undergraduates (SFA1516)				Student financial aid and net price	Student financial aid	1998–1999 to current year	Financial aid to full-time, first-time degree-/certificate-seeking undergraduate students	Total amount of institutional grant aid awarded to full-time first-time undergraduates

Note: Years shown, e.g., EF2015 are examples.

displays quarterly values. It is convenient to set the base year to 100 and then to determine the relative GDP deflator for subsequent years.

Finally, market price in column F, described earlier as the most complicated variable, is computed by subtracting the average institutional grant to first-year full-time students from the average in- and out-of-state tuition and fees. Once that is determined, a GDP deflator must be applied to cast the price for each year in constant (real) base year dollars. The IPEDS sources for the construction of this variable are displayed in table A.8.

Once all the data are obtained and these data, plus the threshold values, which are provided in rows 18 and 19 of the table A.6 template, are entered into the worksheet, then a series of calculations—shown here as Excel formulas—must be completed. The component subscores are derived in rows 15 to 17, the total risk score for each component in row 20, and, finally, F21 displays total Market Stress Test Score for your institution.

Two-Year Public Market Risk Test Score Computation

As you will remember, three components are employed for assessing market stress, that is, for producing the Market Stress Test Score for a Two-Year Public institution. Two of those are relatively straightforward while one requires computation. The enrollment component, first-time enrollment, is the easiest to reproduce and needs only an IPEDS reference. The state and local appropriation values are those directly reported to IPEDS, but for the risk analysis a GDP deflator is applied to cast the sum of these values in constant base year dollars. The ratio of tuition income to instructional expense requires consulting both the income and expense parts of IPEDS' finance data. Later in this section, table A.10 and table A.11 provide directions to the specific IPEDS variables and any special computation needed to produce the components.

After you have chosen the time frame for calculating risk, you need to set up a worksheet or spreadsheet that resembles the template in table A.9. The data entered into table A.9 cover an eight-year period with the earliest year labeled "Base Year" and the last year labeled "Most Recent Year." The three components are shown in columns C to F, row 1.

The data in column C, rows 2 through 9 are the first-time enrollments for the fall of each year. As is specified in table A.10, which illustrates the source of the variable for a sample year, the IPEDS definition for this column is all entering undergraduates. The data section of column D

Table A.9. Worksheet for Two-Year Public institutions

	Excel Row	B	C	D	E
		Excel Column			
	1		First-time	State & local appropriations in constant base year dollars	Ratio of tuition income to instructional expense
Data zone	2	Base year = Year 1	N	$	Ratio
	3	Year 2	N	$	Ratio
	4	Year 3	N	$	Ratio
	5	Year 4	N	$	Ratio
	6	Year 5	N	$	Ratio
	7	Year 6	N	$	Ratio
	8	Year 7	N	$	Ratio
	9	Most recent year = Year 8	N	$	Ratio
Computation zone	10	% change recent vs. base	=(C9-C2)/C2	=(D9-D2)/D2	=(E9-E2)/E2
	11	Slope of line	=SLOPE (C2:C9, A2:A9)	=SLOPE (D2:D9, A2:A9)	=SLOPE (E2:E9, A2:A9)
	12	Intercept of line	=INTERCEPT (C2:C9, A2:A9)	=INTERCEPT (D2:D9, A2:A9)	=INTERCEPT (E2:E9, A2:A9)
	13	Projected value most recent year + 3	C12+(11*C11)	D12+(11*D11)	E12+(11*E11)
	14	% change projected year vs. base year	=(C13-C2)/C2	=(D13-D2)/D2	=(E13-E2)/E2
Testing zone	15	% change recent year vs. base year reaches or falls below alert value	=if(C10<=C18,1,0)	=if(D10<=D18,1,0)	=if(E10<=E18,1,0)
	16	% change recent year vs. base year reaches or falls below warning value	=if(C10<=C19,1,0)	=if(D10<=D19,1,0)	=if(E10<=E19,1,0)
	17	% change projected year vs. base year reaches or falls below alert value	=if(C14<=C18,1,0)	=if(D14<=D18,1,0)	=if(E14<=E18,1,0)
Thresholds	18	Alert value	−29.2%	−19.8%	−28.3%
	19	Warning value	−42.4%	−27.9%	−38.4%
Results	20	Market risk score	=C15+C16+C17	=D15+D16+D17	=E15+E16+E17
	21	Total Market Stress Test Score			=C20+D20+E20

Table A.10. Two-Year Public institutions IPEDS variables and formulas for computing risk scores for first-time enrollment and appropriations

Component		IPEDS variable	Constant dollars	Component variable	IPEDS category	Subcategories			
First-time		Total entering students at the under-graduate level fall 2016 (EF2016D)		Change over time using IPEDS variable	Retention rates, entering class and student-to-faculty ratio	Total entering class	Fall 2001 to current year	Total entering students in the fall, at the undergraduate level	
Appropriations	A	State appropriations (F1516_F1A)	State and local appropriations (A+B) / GDP deflator fall 2016 × 100	Change in real appropria-tions over time	Finance	Public institutions – GASB 34/35	FY 2002 to current	Revenues and other additions	State appropriations
	B	Local appropriations education district taxes and similar support (F1516_F1A)							Local appropriations, education district taxes, and similar support

Note: Years shown, e.g., EF2016D are examples. IPEDS = Integrated Postsecondary Education Data System.

Table A.11. Two-Year Public institutions IPEDS variables and formulas for computing risk scores for tuition income to instructional expense

Component		IPEDS variable	Component variable	IPEDS category	Subcategories			
Tuition income / instructional costs	A	Tuition & fees minus discounts & allowances & institutional fin aid (F1516_F1A)	Change over time of ratio: (A – B) / C	Finance	Public institutions GASB 34/35	Revenues and other additions	FY 2002 to current	Tuition and fees, after deducting discounts and allowances
	B	Institutional grants from unrestricted resources (F1516_F1A)		Finance	Public institutions GASB 34/35	Scholarships and fellowships	FY 2002 to current	Institutional grants from unrestricted resources
	C	Instruction - Current year total (F1516_F1A)		Finance	Public institutions GASB 34/35	Expenses by functional and natural classification: fiscal years 2002 to 2015 / Expenses and salaries and wages by function and total expenses by natural classification: Fiscal years 2016 to current year	FY 2002 to current	Instruction - Current year total

Note: Years shown, e.g., F1516_F1A, are examples. IPEDS = Integrated Postsecondary Education Data System.

requires entering the state and local appropriations per your IPEDS submission. However, the annual value of the combined appropriations needs to be converted to real, that is, constant base year dollars. A good source for the GDP deflator is https://fred.stlouisfed.org/series/GDPDEF since it displays quarterly values. It is convenient to set the base year to 100 and then to determine the relative GDP deflator for subsequent years.

Turning to column E, the data here require computations using several IPEDS variables from the submitted finance data. The specific data and where they are found in IPEDS is delineated in table A.11.

Once all the data are obtained and these data, plus the threshold values, which are provided in rows 18 and 19 of the table A.9 template, are entered into the worksheet, then a series of calculations—shown here as Excel formulas—must be completed. The component subscores are derived in rows 15 to 17, the total score for each component in row 20, and finally, E21 displays the Market Stress Test Score for your institution.

On Squaring the Circle

Providing a detailed map of the shifts in undergraduate enrollments across the United States is always an exercise in uncertainty. The basic data come from the National Center for Education Statistics' (NCES) Integrated Postsecondary Education Data System (IPEDS) and is supplied by the more than 3,800 postsecondary institutions whose students are eligible to participate in a federal financial aid program, are located in one of the 50 states, grant an undergraduate degree, and whose programs are not 100 percent distance education. All enumerations of postsecondary enrollments are in fact summations of a set of individual reports submitted to IPEDS by federally eligible postsecondary institutions. Over the last decade, IPEDS has gone to considerable lengths to improve the quality of the data that the institutions have supplied and NCES has subsequently made publicly available. Most institutions take seriously their mandated reporting requirements, but inevitably a small volume of inconsistent data creeps in. At the same time, a variety of institutions submit incomplete reports at least some of the time. IPEDS itself periodically changes the definitions of individual data elements, occasionally making comparisons across time problematic. We should note, as well, that some data elements are submitted every other year rather than every year.

In order to construct a reliable database detailing postsecondary enrollments across the United States from 2008 to 2016, we developed two lists of postsecondary institutions supplying data to IPEDS. The first was a master list of institutions that met the criteria just listed, were not seminaries, and reported enrollment of more than 100 degree- or certificate-seeking undergraduates in 2016. In addition, institutions with missing data or clearly inconsistent data were eliminated yielding a total of 3,517 institutions. Summing the submitted reports from this set of institutions yields an estimate of undergraduate enrollments for 2016 of 14,992,208.

We then developed a second list of institutions, as a subset of the first, that we have labeled the core list. This list includes only institutions whose IPEDS submissions for 2008, 2011, and 2016 allow us to identify each institution's market segment, market price, and ethnic profile for each of these years. Altogether, 2,853 institutions met these criteria. In 2016, enrollments in their undergraduate degree and certificate programs totaled 14,113,065. These enrollments represent 94 percent of the equivalent enrollments reported by all institutions on the master institutional list.

The detailed analysis of Market Stress Test Scores reported in this book used a third subset, which excluded all Private For-Profit institutions and Two-Year Private Not-for-Profit institutions.

A more complete understanding of the profile of institutions included on this further reduced list of institutions emerges when the analysis is disaggregated by sector and institutional type. In our analysis, we reclassified 122 predominantly Two-Year Public institutions that IPEDS had shifted to the Four-Year Public category because they awarded some baccalaureate degrees. Tables B.1, B.2, and B.3 report the number of Four-Year Public, Two-Year Public, and Four-Year Private Not-for-Profit institutions in our analysis and their enrollments as reported to IPEDS.

Table B.1. Four-Year Public institutions (less 122 reclassified Two-Year Public institutions)

	Master list	Core list less 122 reclassified Two-Year Publics	With Market Risk Score
Institutions	735	552	490
Enrollments	6,833,731	5,695,408	5,487,464
Percentage of reclassified enrollments			96%

Table B.2. Two-Year Public institutions (plus 122 reclassified as Four-Year Public institutions)

	Master list	Core list plus 122 reclassified as Four-Year Publics	With Market Risk Score
Institutions	894	988	930
Enrollments	4,714,728	5,504,407	5,320,241
Percentage of reclassified enrollments			97%

Table B.3. Four-Year Private Not-for-Profit institutions

	Master list	Core list	With Market Risk Score
Institutions	1,394	1,003	900
Enrollments	2,726,149	2,448,299	2,208,500
Percentage of core list enrollments			90%

Enrollments are themselves a subset of the market in that they include only students who enrolled and not those who might have considered enrolling but didn't. In other words, our estimates of the size of the markets for undergraduate education in the United States are estimates of buyers, not shoppers.

A Note on Verification

Just as we were completing this volume Wheeling Jesuit University declared financial exigency. Its president, Michael Mihalyo, told his campus that the institution no longer had the resources "to bridge the gap between highly discounted enrollments, associated academic and athletic programming costs, and the revenue needed to support the institution's operational expenses" (Toppo 2019). And there, in a single sentence, was an unexpected catalog of the variables that we made central to our Market Stress Test Score methodology.

Which brings us to the question, "Could we verify our methodology more systematically?" In the text, we noted that there were not enough closures to develop a statistical model that would best predict which institutions were likely to close. However, we could ask, "What were the Market Stress Test Scores of those institutions that have closed since 2016?" The most complete, regularly updated list of college and university closures, mergers, and consolidations is compiled by Education Dive (2019), a subsidiary of Industry Dive. That list of closures included 12 private, not-for-profit institutions that had closed (or that had announced impending closure) and for which we could calculate a Market Stress Test Score. Of the 12 institutions, 9 were in the substantial risk category (Market Stress Test Score ≥ 4), and of these, 5 had scores greater or equal to 6, indicating severe stress just prior to or in anticipation of closing. Not one was in the minimal risk zone—a Market Stress Test Score of 0 or 1 (table C.1).

The Education Dive list includes institutions that merged with another stronger institution after 2016; for three of those institutions we could calculate a Market Stress Test Score (table C.2). All three institutions were facing substantial risk in 2016 just prior to their mergers.

A third potential confirmation of our methodology is available because the federal government requires private not-for-profit institutions to

Table C.1. Education Dive list of closings with corresponding Market Stress Test Scores

Institution	Region	Year	Market Stress Test Score
Green Mountain College	New England	2019	9
Concordia College Alabama (HBCU)	Southeast	2018	8
Newbury College	New England	2019	7
Marygrove College	Great Lakes	2018	6
Grace University	Plains	2018	6
College of Saint Joseph	New England	2019	5
College of New Rochelle	Mid-Atlantic	2014	4
St. Joseph's (IN)	Great Lakes	2017	4
St. Gregory's University	Southwest	2017	4
Southern Vermont College	New England	2019	3
Memphis College of Art	Southeast	2020	2
Mount Ida College	New England	2018	2

HBCU = historically black college and university.

Table C.2. Education Dive list of mergers with corresponding Market Stress Test Scores

Institution	Region	Year	Market Stress Test Score
New Hampshire Institute of Art	New England	2019	8
Thomas Jefferson University	Mid-Atlantic	2017	5
Wheelock College	New England	2018	4

Table C.3. Financial Responsibility Composite Score compared to Market Stress Test Score

Financial Responsibility Composite Score	Mean Market Stress Test Score
>1.5	1.8
1.0–1.5	3.2
<1.0	3.4

submit audited financial statements annually to the US Department of Education to demonstrate they are maintaining the standards of financial responsibility necessary to participate in the Title IV programs. The analysis the department performs results in a Financial Responsibility Composite Score for each submitting institution reflecting the relative financial health of the institution along a scale from negative 1.0 to positive 3.0. A score greater than or equal to 1.5 indicates the institution is considered financially responsible. Institutions with scores of less than 1.5 but greater than or equal to 1.0 are considered financially responsible but requiring additional oversight. A college or university with a score less than 1.0 is considered not financially responsible. In general, institutions rated as facing financial difficulties (composite score less than 1.5) were also likely to be facing market stress as measured by our Market Stress Test Scores (table C.3).

Ultimately, only time will tell whether our Market Stress Test Score identifies institutions likely to face closing or a merger.

Allen, Robert W. 2019. "Message from the President." Green Mountain College. Accessed April 30, 2019. https://www.greenmtn.edu/message-from-the -president/.

Armitage, Andrew S. 2018. "Outcomes of Tuition Resets at Small Private, Not-for-Profit Institutions." EdD diss., University of Pennsylvania.

Booth, Olivia, and Timothy Bolger. 2016. "Dowling College Abruptly Closing, Sparking Sadness, Anger." *Long Island Press*, June 3. https://www .longislandpress.com/2016/06/03/dowling-college-abruptly-closing-sparking -sadness-anger/.

Carapezza, Kirk. 2018. "Former Mount Ida Students Sue Administrators for Fraud." WGBH News, November 26. https://www.wgbh.org/news/education /2018/11/26/former-mount-ida-students-sue-administrators-for-fraud.

Casamento, Laura. 2016. "A Multiple Case Study Analysis Exploring How Less Selective Tuition-Dependent Colleges and Universities Approached an Undergraduate Tuition Price Reset Strategy." EdD diss., University of Pennsylvania.

Chingos, Matthew. 2018. "America's Education 'Deserts' Show Limits of Relaxing Regulations on Colleges." *New York Times*, August 14. https://www .nytimes.com/2018/08/14/upshot/education-free-market-regulation-problems .html.

Czerniewicz, Laura, and Sukaina Walji. 2019. "Issues for Universities Using Private Companies for Online Education." Centre for Innovation in Learning and Teaching (CILT), University of Cape Town. Accessed April 30, 2019. https://open.uct.ac.za/handle/11427/29813.

Dudley, Will. 2018. "A Message from President Dudley." Washington and Lee University, May 14. https://www.wlu.edu/presidents-office/issues-and -initiatives/strategic-planning/a-message-from-president-dudley.

Education Dive. 2019. "How Many Colleges Have Closed Since 2016?" Education Dive, March 29. https://www.educationdive.com/news/tracker -college-and-university-closings-and-consolidation/539961/.

Frey, Thomas. 2013. "By 2030 50% of Colleges Will Collapse." *Futurist Speaker* (blog), July 5. https://futuristspeaker.com/business-trends/by-2030-over-50-of -colleges-will-collapse/.

Harris, Adam. 2018. "Here's How Higher Education Dies." *The Atlantic*, June 5. https://www.theatlantic.com/education/archive/2018/06/heres-how-higher -education-dies/561995/.

Howe, Jeff. 2013. "Clayton Christensen Wants to Transform Capitalism." *Wired*, February 12. https://www.wired.com/2013/02/mf-clayton-christensen -wants-to-transform-capitalism/.

Jacobs, Peter. 2015. "'U Failed Us!'—For-Profit College Students Plaster Campus with Angry Posters after Abrupt Closure." *Business Insider*, April 27. https://www.businessinsider.com/u-failed-us-for-profit-college-students-plaster -campus-with-angry-posters-after-abrupt-closure-2015-4.

Jaschik, Scott. 2018. "Are Prospective Students about to Disappear?" *Inside Higher Ed*, January 8. https://www.insidehighered.com/admissions/article /2018/01/08/new-book-argues-most-colleges-are-about-face-significant -decline.

———. 2019. "Another Small College Will Close." *Inside Higher Ed*, January 24. https://www.insidehighered.com/news/2019/01/24/green-mountain -latest-small-college-close.

Koretsky, Carla M. 2017. "Strategic Planning—Dean's Announcement." College of Arts and Sciences, Western Michigan University. Accessed April 30, 2019. https://wmich.edu/arts-sciences/deans-message.

Krantz, Laura. 2018a. "Former Mount Ida College Students and Staff Are Trying to Move Forward." *Boston Globe*, November 22. https://www .bostonglobe.com/metro/2018/11/22/former-mount-ida-students-professors -pick-pieces/9KmZGG01ZRnnciJnO7WKrM/story.html.

———. 2018b. "'Why Are You Preying on Our Children?': Fury over Mount Ida Closing at Hearing." *Boston Globe*, April 24. https://www.bostonglobe .com/metro/2018/04/24/why-are-you-preying-our-children-fury-over-mount -ida-closure-hearing/97KvJfvzSoocsft9dc8DiJ/story.html.

Lederman, Doug. 2017. "Clay Christensen, Doubling Down." *Inside Higher Ed*, April 28. https://www.insidehighered.com/digital-learning/article/2017/04/28 /clay-christensen-sticks-predictions-massive-college-closures.

———. 2018. "Peril for Small Private Colleges: A Survey of Business Officers." *Inside Higher Ed*, July 20. https://www.insidehighered.com/news/survey/peril -private-colleges-survey-business-officers.

———. 2019. "The Mood Brightens: A Survey of Presidents." *Inside Higher Ed*, March 8. http://www.insidehighered.com/news/survey/2019-survey-college -and-university-presidents.

Leef, George. 2018. "The College Bubble Begins to Deflate." *National Review*, July 6. https://www.nationalreview.com/corner/the-college-bubble-begins-to -deflate/.

Lindsay, Drew. 2018. "The $44-Million Rescue." *Chronicle of Higher Education*, March 13. https://www.chronicle.com/article/The-44-Million-Rescue /242743.

Mangan, Katherine. 2018. "Questions Swirl as Earlham College's President Will Leave after Just a Year." *Chronicle of Higher Education*, July 2. https://www .chronicle.com/article/Questions-Swirl-as-Earlham/243821.

McCready, Peggy A. 2013. "Technologically Enhanced Teaching Learning." EdD diss., University of Pennsylvania.

Miller, Vanessa. 2018. "Iowa Wesleyan's Fate Underscores Woes Facing Others." *The Gazette,* November 10. https://www.thegazette.com/subject/news /education/iowa-wesleyan-financial-woes-small-liberal-arts-colleges-problems -20181110.

Nelson, Miriam. 2019. "Letter from President Nelson." Hampshire College, January 15. https://www.hampshire.edu/news/2019/01/15/january-15-2019 -letter-from-president-nelson.

Osei, Zipporah. 2019. "For Alumnae, the Fight to Keep Bennett College Open Is a Fight for Black Women in Academe." *Chronicle of Higher Education,* January 16. https://www.chronicle.com/article/For-Alumnae-the-Fight-to -Keep/245488.

Poderis, Tony. 2019. "How Much Endowment Is 'Right' for Our Organization." Raise-Funds.com. Accessed April 30, 2019. www.raise-funds.com/how-much -endowment-is-right-for-our-organizaton.

Putnam, Mark. 2018. "A Meta-strategy for the Future of Central College." Confidential paper to the Board of Trustees, Central College, IA.

Quick, Michael W. 2018. "The 2018 USC Strategic Plan–Answering the Call." USC Provost, University of Southern California, February 26. https://www .provost.usc.edu/2018-usc-strategic-plan-answering-the call/.

Rensselaer Polytechnic Institute. 2012. "The Mobile Studio Project in Physics." Accessed April 30, 2019. http://www.rpi.edu/dept/phys/MobileProject /Untitled-3.html.

Selingo, Jeffrey J. 2018. "Despite Strong Economy, Worrying Financial Signs for Higher Education." *Washington Post*, April 3. https://www.washingtonpost .com/news/grade-point/wp/2018/08/03/despite-strong-economy-worrying -financial-signs-for-higher-education/?utm_term=.a61f71831586.

Seltzer, Rick. 2017. "Days of Reckoning." *Inside Higher Ed*, November 13. https://www.insidehighered.com/news/2017/11/13/spate-recent-college -closures-has-some-seeing-long-predicted-consolidation-taking.

———. 2018a. "Moody's: Private-College Closures at 11 Per Year." *Inside Higher Ed*, July 25. www.insidehighered.com/quicktakes/2018/07/25/moodys -private-college-closures-11-year.

———. 2018b. "Too Late for a Fix?" *Inside Higher Ed*, August 8. https://www .insidehighered.com/news/2018/08/08/leaked-documents-call-question-saint -augustines-universitys-future.

———. 2019. "Strength in Smaller Numbers?" *Inside Higher Ed*, February 20. https://www.insidehighered.com/news/2019/02/20/presidents-skeptical-some -colleges-closing-can-help-others-survive.

Stripling, Jack. 2019. "Spend. Build. Repeat. Unbridled Growth Is at the Heart of a Crisis at UCF." *Chronicle of Higher Education,* February 20. https://www .chronicle.com/article/Spend-Build-Repeat/245740?cid=trend_right_a.

Svrluga, Susan. 2016. "Alumnae Vowed to Save Sweet Briar from Closing Last Year. And They Did." *Washington Post*, March 3. https://www.washingtonpost .com/news/grade-point/wp/2016/03/03/alumnae-vowed-to-save-sweet-briar -from-closing-last-year-and-they-did/?utm_term=.c695c9e989b5.

Toppo, Greg. 2019. "Wheeling Jesuit Declares Financial Exigency." #Quick Takes. *Inside Higher Ed*, March 12. https://www.insidehighered.com /quicktakes/2019/03/12/wheeling-jesuit-declares-financial-exigency.

Vahey, Karen. 2019. "The Market for Undergraduate Admissions." Unpublished paper, Executive Doctorate in Higher Education Management, University of Pennsylvania.

Walsh, Colleen. 2018. "Two Leaders, One Harvard." *Harvard Gazette*, May 22. https://news.harvard.edu/gazette/story/2018/05/drew-faust-and-larry-bacow -on-learning-from-each-other/.

White, Byron P. 2016. "The Myth of the College-Ready Student." *Inside Higher Ed*, March 21. https://www.insidehighered.com/views/2016/03/21/instead -focusing-college-ready-students-institutions-should-become-more-student.

Zemsky, Robert. 2013. *Checklist for Change: Making American Higher Education a Sustainable Enterprise*. New Brunswick, NJ: Rutgers University Press.

Zemsky, Robert, and Penney Oedel. 1983. *The Structure of College Choice*. Princeton, NJ: The College Board.

Zemsky, Robert, and Susan Shaman. 2017. *The Market Imperative: Segmentation and Change in Higher Education*. Baltimore: Johns Hopkins University Press.

Zemsky, Robert, Susan Shaman, and Daniel B. Shapiro. 2001. *Higher Education as Competitive Enterprise: When Markets Matter*. San Francisco: Jossey-Bass.

Page numbers in *italics* refer to figures and tables.

enrollments: actual, 22, 23; changes in, over time, 21, 21, 23; competition for, within sectors, 23–27; diminished, distribution of, 28–29, 37; as factor in Market Stress Test Score, 40–41, 41, 44, 46, 51; market sector and market risk by, 58, 58–59; by market segment, 23–25, 25–26, 27; as reflected in IPEDS, 21; state market examples of, 32–34, 33; trends in, 19–20, 27–28; tuition resets and, 98–102

ethnicity of undergraduates: in institutions at substantial risk, 82; by sector, 32, 32; by sector and risk, 66, 66–67

faculty productivity, increases in, 102–6

federal grants to institutions, 67, 67, 69

financial risk and market risk, 117

financial status of institutions: as factor in Market Stress Test Score, 52; mapping, 3; measurement of, 41–43, 45, 46; U.S. Department of Education ratings of, 144, 144–45

flipping curriculum, 109–10

for-profit providers, 19. *See also* Four-Year Private For-Profit sector

Four-Year Private For-Profit sector: age of students in, 31; as disrupted portion of market, 57; enrollments in, 21, 21, 22, 23, 30; median retention rate for, 106–7; substantial risks faced by, 82

Four-Year Private Not-for-Profit sector: assignment of Market Stress Test Score for, 50; computation of Market Stress Test Score for, 122, 123–27, 128; database of institutions in, 141; enrollments in, 21, 22, 23, 26, 27; geographic region and enrollments in, 30; market price and enrollments in, 84–85, 84–86, 86; market risk for, 61, 61–63, 62; market segment and enrollments in, 29; Market Stress Test Score for, 40–43, 41, 42, 44, 56; Medallions in, 71–72, 72, 73; size and enrollments in, 29–30; substantial risks faced by, 75–78, 76, 77, 78

Four-Year Public sector: assignment of Market Stress Test Score for, 51;

computation of Market Stress Test Score for, 128, 129–32, 137; database of institutions in, 140; enrollments in, 21, 22, 23, 25, 27; geographic region and enrollments in, 29; market risk in, 59–60, 59–61; market segment and enrollments in, 28; Market Stress Test Score for, 43–45, 45, 56; Medallions in, 72–73, 73; median retention rate for, 106; size and enrollments in, 28–29; substantial risks faced by, 78–80, 79–80, 81. *See also* state appropriations

Frey, Tom, 5

Gates, Jeff, 111–12

GDP (gross domestic product) deflator, 122

general education courses, recasting, 108–10

geographic region: enrollment shifts by, 25–26, 27, 29; overview of, 23; state market examples of, 32–34, 33; urban vs. rural, 35–36

geographic region and market risk: for Four-Year Private Not-for-Profit sector, 61, 61–62; for Four-Year Public sector, 59, 59; for Two-Year Public sector, 63, 63–64

Good Buy segment, 24

Good Opportunity segment, 24, 29

graduation rates: Convenience and Good Opportunity segments and, 61; improving, 107; market segment and, 25; rank and, 24, 36

Grawe, Nathan, 8

Green Mountain College, 14, 16

grief, language of, in talk about higher education, 14–17

Hampshire College, 15

Harris, Adam, 4

Hartman, Joel, 104–5

Heald College, 16

"Here's How Higher Education Dies" (Harris), 4

higher education, language of conversations about: alerts and warnings, 39–40; elegiac grief, 14–17; overview of, 6–7; reassurance, 10–14; threat, 7–10. *See also* undergraduate education

Higher Education as Competitive Enterprise (Zemsky, Shaman, and Shapiro), 96–97

Hispanic students: enrollments of, 32, 32; by market sector and risk, 66, 67

indicators of outcomes for law schools, 2

Inside Higher Ed: annual surveys of, 12–13; on closure of Green Mountain College, 14

institutional size and enrollments, 23, 25–26, 27, 28–29

institutional size and market risk: for Four-Year Private Not-for-Profit sector, 62, 62–63; for Four-Year Public sector, 60, 60; for Two-Year Public sector, 64, 64–65

institutional viability: emotions related to questions of, 4, 14–17; model for, 2–3; overview of, 3; risk score for quantification of, 39. *See also* Market Stress Test Score

institutions: levers for altering future of, 95–96; merged, Market Stress Test Score for, 143. *See also* closures of institutions; financial status of institutions; institutional viability; rural institutions; struggling institutions; urban institutions; *specific institutions*

instructional costs, reduction in, 102–6

Iowa, enrollments in, 33, 33–34

Iowa Wesleyan, 10

IPEDS (Integrated Postsecondary Education Data System): database constructed from data in, 20–21, 139–41, 140–41; limitations of data in, 52–53; overview of, 3; residency data in, 44; tuition discount in, 42–43; use of, in analysis, 119, 120

journalists, stories told by, 9–10

Kaplan University, 57

Learning Alliance for Higher Education, The, 96

legal education, market for, 2

liberal education, 11, 108

losers in consolidating markets, risks faced by, 75–76, 75–80, 77, 78, 79–80, 81

mappings of institutional stress test scores, 3

market: definition of, 94; disruption of, evidence for, 65; as fixed, 93, 94; importance of understanding, 1–2; for legal education, 2; need for discussion of, 116–17; rigidity of, 37. *See also* consolidating market; Four-Year Private For-Profit sector; Four-Year Private Not-for-Profit sector; Four-Year Public sector; Two-Year Public sector

Market Imperative, The (Zemsky and Shaman), 3, 23–24, 97, 120

market price: as financial measure, 41–43, 42; for public institutions, 44; for struggling institutions, 84–85, 84–86, 86. *See also* pricing strategies

market risk: analysis of data on, 65–66; enrollment and distribution of, 58, 58–59; financial risk and, 117; in Four-Year Private Not-for-Profit sector, 61, 61–62; in Four-Year Public sector, 59–60, 59–61; identification of, 93; maldistribution of, 67–69; in Two-Year Public sector, 63, 63–65, 64. *See also* risk of institutional closures

market segment and enrollments, 23–25, 25–26, 27

market segment and market risk: for Four-Year Not-for-Profit sector, 61, 61–63, 62; for Four-Year Private Not-for-Profit sector, 62, 63; for Four-Year Public sector, 60, 61

market segments. *See* Convenience segment; Good Buy segment; Good Opportunity segment; Medallion segment; Name Brand segment

market stress for law schools, 2

Market Stress Test Score: application of, 119; assignment of, 49, 49–51; for Central College, 113, 113;

risk categories for, *64, 64–65;* urban institutions compared to, *35–36, 36*

Rutgers University-Newark, Honors College at, 107–8

Saint Augustine University, 9

Selingo, Jeff, 8

shoppers, converting to buyers, 94

slope of trend lines, 48–49, 96–97

Southern New Hampshire University, 65–66

spreadsheet programs, 119

state appropriations: as financial measure, 45, *45,* 46–47, *47;* moderate risk related to, *87–88, 87–90, 89,* 94; substantial risk related to, 65, 79, 81; for University of Central Florida, 104

strategies, rejuvenating: at Central College, 112–16; marketing and retention, 106–10; origins of, 96–97; pricing, 97–106, 111–12; at Utica College, 110–12

Structure of College Choice, The (Zemsky and Oedel), 96

struggling institutions: community colleges, 90, *91, 91;* consistency of challenges faced by, 91–92; overview of, 117; private, *84–85, 84–86, 86;* public, *87–88, 87–90, 89*

students: competition for, within sectors, 23–27; economic resources of, by sector and risk, 67, *67. See also* demographic characteristics of students; ethnicity of undergraduates; graduation rates; retention, first-year to second-year

Studio Physics, 102–3

SUNY colleges and universities, 88

Sweet Briar College, 9, 14, 15–16

Tatum, Beverly, 107

technology to reduce instructional costs, 102–6

threat, language of, in talk about higher education, 7–10

time frame for analysis, 120, 122

Title IV-eligible colleges and universities, 20–21

trend lines, slope of, 48–49, 96–97

tuition: discounts of, 42–43, 81–82; income from, 46, 47; resets of, 98–102, 111–12

Two-Year Public sector: adult learners in, 32; assignment of Market Stress Test Score for, *52;* computation of Market Stress Test Score for, 133, *134–36,* 137; database of institutions in, *140;* ebb and flow of enrollments in, 82, 90, *91;* enrollments in, 21, *21,* 22, *23,* 26–27; geographic region and enrollments in, 30; market risk for, *63, 63–65, 64;* Market Stress Test Score for, 45–47, *47,* 56, 75; Medallions in, *74, 74,* 81; size and enrollments in, 30; substantial risks faced by, *75–76, 78*

undergraduate education: expansion of market for, 19–20, 27–28; sectors of, 20–21; value proposition of, 117. *See also* Four-Year Private For-Profit sector; Four-Year Public sector; Two-Year Public sector

University of Central Florida (UCF), 103–6

University of Michigan, 44–45

University of Phoenix, 57

University of Texas, 44–45

University of Virginia, 44–45

University of Wisconsin Oshkosh, 108–9

urban institutions: risk categories for, *64, 64–65;* rural institutions compared to, *35–36, 36*

U.S. Department of Education, Financial Responsibility Composite Scores, *144,* 144–45

U.S. News & World Report rankings, 24, 36

Utica College, 98, 99, 110–12, *111,* 115–16

Vahey, Karen, *111*

warnings: law school admissions market, 2; thresholds for, 47–48

Wheeling Jesuit University, 143

White, Byron, 107–8

Wilson, Jack, 103

winners in consolidating markets, 71–74, *72, 73, 74*